PEARLS OF WISDOM

Be Truly Set Free!

TERRY SWEENEY

Copyright © 2020 by Terry Sweeney All rights reserved.

No part of this book may be reproduced, copied, stored or transmitted in any form or by any means - graphic, electronic or mechanical, including photocopying, without the prior written permission of Ann Fitzpatrick and Little Doves except where permitted by law. Exceptions are made for brief excerpts used in published reviews.

ISBN 13: 978-1-7359006-0-5
ISBN 10: 1-7359006-0-5

Published by Terry Sweeney www.terrysweeney.com
Cover Design by Eowyn Riggins
Interior Layout by Rachel Greene

Front Cover Photo: The Dancing Sun in Medjugorje, Bosnia and Herzegovina
Back Cover Photo: St. James Church in Medjugorje, Bosnia and Herzegovina

Printed in the United States of America

I would like to thank our Lord Jesus Christ for His, love, mercy and strength for the journey. — T.S.

CONTENTS

Foreword	i
Prologue	iii
Chapter One	1
Secrets	
Chapter Two	13
It's None of Your Business What Other People Think About You	
Chapter Three	21
Don't Die Wondering	
Chapter Four	29
Patience/Humility	
Chapter Five	35
You've Got to Give It Up to Keep It	
Chapter Six	41
Acceptance	
Chapter Seven	45
Heroes/Role Models	

Chapter Eight	51
Are You the Best?	
Chapter Nine	59
Pornography	
Chapter Ten	65
Anger	
Chapter Eleven	75
Prejudice	
Chapter Twelve	79
Ego	
Chapter Thirteen	83
Peace	
Chapter Fourteen	89
Forgiveness	
Chapter Fifteen	103
Surrender Without Giving Up	
Chapter Sixteen	109
Amends	
Chapter Seventeen	119
Insecurity	
Chapter Eighteen	127
Fear	
Chapter Nineteen	137
Fidelity	

Chapter Twenty	143
Guilt	
Chapter Twenty-One	147
Resentments	
Chapter Twenty-Two	155
Fellowship	
Chapter Twenty-Three	167
Listening	
Chapter Twenty-Four	173
What Do You Stand For?	
Chapter Twenty-Five	185
Trust	
Chapter Twenty-Six	189
Goals and the Subconscious Mind	
Chapter Twenty-Seven	197
Entitlement	
Chapter Twenty-Eight	201
Respect	
Chapter Twenty-Nine	209
God	
Chapter Thirty	219
Shame	
Chapter Thirty-One	225
Isolation and Loneliness	

Chapter Thirty-Two	231
Attitude	
Chapter Thirty-Three	237
Self-Image	
Chapter Thirty-Four	245
Life	
Epilogue	253
About Terry Sweeney	257

FOREWORD

Terry Sweeney is a fascinating guy. His life story is filled with interesting achievements along with the kinds of twists and turns that leave a person either devastated or motivated. In Terry's case, it's clearly the latter. He has done more than make lemonade from the lemons life has at times thrown his way, he has made *Pearls*.

This book is filled with wonderful life-lessons. Lessons learned against the backdrop of a good deal of pain. But Terry doesn't complain. He never got bitter. He got better.

And better and better.

If I could describe Terry in one word it would be: *Authentic*. He is an American original. The real deal. And growing up in Boston, well, that gives him, shall we say, a colorful edge and way of explaining things.

As you read through the following pages, I encourage you to pause at times to let what he says sink in. I also encourage you to take notes, write key thoughts down. Terry is big on this. As Lord Francis Bacon (1561-1626) said: "Reading makes a full man; *Writing makes an exact man.*"

Indeed.

Whether it is the chapter on *Forgiveness* (powerful!), or the one on *Goals*, or his thoughts about *Secrets*, what Terry has to say will touch your heart, challenge your assumptions, and inspire you to become a better person.

What more could you ask for in a book?

David R. Stokes
Fairfax, Virginia

PROLOGUE

I began writing *Pearls of Wisdom* about 17 years ago. I cannot tell you exactly when, as my brain does not work that way. However, I am confident that my ex-wife could tell you the exact date, as her brain *does* work that way. I don't remember much these days. The airways are all polluted with nonsense anyway. Therefore, if someone tells me something and it has no meaning to me, it goes in one ear and out the other without actually registering. Then, if something does register, I have to write it down, as I usually do not remember that stuff, either. As Simon & Garfunkel sang in their song, *The Boxer*: "A man is what he wants to hear and disregards the rest."

In addition, I had no idea what the title of this book was going to be, however one day this year *the light went on*, and "Pearls of Wisdom" came to mind.

Another reason why it took me so long to get my manuscript out of the file cabinet was that between my work as a business owner (a company that helped folks get out of debt through negotiations with their creditors) and being the sole breadwinner for a family with six children, (my wife did not work outside the home) there was little extra time to write, not to mention the incredible stress of just being able to put food on the table for eight people.

So, having been diagnosed with PTSD, depression, and anxiety, but unwilling to take my medications, thinking that I didn't need to take any pills to take care of myself, it made for some very difficult years in my marriage. On top of that, my now ex-wife home-schooled our children. Where she ever got the patience for that, I will never know. But she did a beautiful job, and all of them went off to college.

Therefore, this fledgling book sat in my file cabinet and lingered on my laptop. I eventually asked one of my sisters if she would edit it for me, and she did a great job, as well. However, she wanted to add her own two cents into my book. I told her that as an editor, you cannot do that. If you have something to say, write your own book! However, I am grateful for what she did.

After she did her edits, the manuscript sadly went back into the file cabinet. I tell you this—this is for other would-be authors out there, because telling your story is so important today, just as it was in the old days. I will never forget the day my mother told me that no matter how hard you try, you will never be able to read all of the books you want to. She was right about that. Of course, I never knew I was going the have to run my own company, while at the same time providing for a family of eight people. The good news is, by the grace of God, and only by the grace of God, did we make it.

I then went online to see 1.) If the web domain for this book had been taken. It had, and 2.) If there were any other books in existence with the same title. The first one that I saw was by former First Lady, Barbara Bush. I'm willing to bet that that is a great book as well. I just don't think I'll have the time to read it, as my mother said, back when I was about ten.

But get this—I recently had to have surgery on my nose for basal cell cancer. This was the second time I have had to have this done on my face. I guess I am my own worst enemy. I drive a convertible and put the top down 90% of the time. In addition, I used to go to tanning salons in my early 30s. So, after the dermatologist was done frying off the skin on my nose, (just the smell of someone's burning skin is terrible enough), and she *got it all*, you then go in to see the plastic surgeon, who attempts to put my face, or nose in my case, back together again.

Good luck with that this time, as I literally had a crater on my nose. Anyway, I was telling the plastic surgeon about this book, and the title of Mrs. Bush's volume. He told me that he had actually done some similar work on Mrs. Bush as well. I asked him; "What are the odds, that the same plastic surgeon helped two authors, whose books have the exact same name?" I then said to him, "You're notorious." To which he replied jokingly, "I already know that."

Anyway, earlier this year, I decided it was time to hang up my company business ties. All of my children are out of the house now. So, I went to the file cabinet, pulled out the file with a label that read, simply, "book," and decided to complete it.

And what an adventure this has been! Oh my gosh. I had no idea what the journey would be like, from actually writing the book, to getting the ISBN number, to editing, to publishing, etc., and all the other steps in between that go into getting a book from my computer, onto the shelves of the people who sell your books. Just an incredible journey.

At least when I write my next book—The Hollywood Marine, about my adventures in the Marine Corps—I will be better acquainted with all the working parts, from writing, to editing, to publishing, etc.

Now it's time for the book. I really do trust you will enjoy reading *Pearls of Wisdom*. I had to make a lot of edits, as many things have changed over the last 17 years since I first started writing this, just as they will change over the next 17 years. I hope by then our Lord calls me home, because I really do not think I want to live past 80. I'm in enough physical pain from past injuries, including having to eject from an RF-4 one night when I was in the Marines. As a result, I already feel like I am in the ninth inning anyway! And, I started taking my meds as directed about six years ago. I wish I had done that a lot earlier. It might have saved my marriage. Just another example of how powerful **a man's** bravado/ego can be.

So, I do hope you enjoy this work, and hopefully you will take the time to write to me at www.terrysweeney.com about anything and everything you read.

May God bless you always.

Terry Sweeney
Laguna Beach, CA
September 2020

CHAPTER ONE
Secrets

"I thought about how there are two types of secrets: the kind you want to keep in, and the kind you don't dare to let out." — Ally Carter

Okay, so here we go. I have elected to write this chapter about secrets first, as I feel this could help so many people, right now, today if you want it to! In fact, if you never read any more of this book and just did this one exercise, you would be light years ahead of your peers.

I have been so blessed by so many people in my life and the wisdom they have passed down to me. Therefore, I have decided to share as much of that wisdom with as many readers as possible.

While doing some research for this book, I would ask various people if they had any secrets. Not usually a great conversation starter, but I did learn a few surprising things. For example, when I asked random women if they had any secrets, I never came across one—not a single one—who didn't admit to having secrets. "Of course, I do." Or, "Who doesn't?" Or, "Everybody has secrets." These were the three most common responses I received from women. Not one of them denied having secrets! On the other hand, when I asked men the same question, I'd get a look like I was among the fish swimming in a giant aquarium. Either they wouldn't admit to harboring any secrets, or they'd just shrug the question off.

We all have secrets. You do. I used to.

If I may, let me tell you a story about my secrets. On my 30th birthday, I walked into one of those 12-step meeting groups. It turned out to be the first time in my life that I truly felt "at home." I understood what the people in the group were talking about. Well, except for one lady who shared about talking to God while sitting on the toilet that morning. The point is that I understood what they were talking about. And they understood what I was talking about. By the time the meeting was over, I walked out crying.

But it was a good kind of cry, if you know what I mean.

That was a key moment in my life. I started to learn about 12-step groups in general and the 12 steps that are *recommended* in order to help you with whatever addiction you are fraught with. And the best part was, I could follow along with them all at my own pace. No pressure.

I really liked that part.

I knocked out the first three steps fairly easily, but the fourth one slowed me down big time. It's the one that says, *"Made a searching and fearless moral inventory of ourselves."* I could tell right away that this one was going to give me some trouble.

I should also mention that these programs strongly recommend having someone to sponsor you—a mentor of sorts—somebody to hold your hand, so to speak. So, I approached the man I perceived to be the president of the group—his name was Roy—for assistance in finding someone to help me with this step. He assured me that I would find somebody that could help me and even offered to be my sponsor until I found someone myself.

Roy was about ten years older than I was, but even in his 40s he had a kind of sage-like wisdom—like that of a man in his 80s. A short, mildly-pudgy man, he was like one of those little teddy bears found in hospital gift shops. A lovable guy who was easy to talk to. In fact, he was a great listener, which is probably why I found it easy to share my story with him. I told him about my struggles, how I was trying to better my life, which up to that point had been a tornado, physically, mentally, spiritually, and emotionally. Now I had to learn how to live on life's terms, not on Terry's terms. I fully admit, I did not like that term, "living life on life's terms."

Roy was a fascinating guy who had also been quite a gambler. He ended up being my accountant, as well. One day I was in his office not far from John Wayne Airport in Orange County, and he said to me, "Terry, whenever I want to, I can pick up the phone, call a guy in Las Vegas, and he'll send a private jet over here to pick me up within an hour."

So, I guess he was a high-roller, too.

During one of my early conversations with Roy, the subject of secrets came up. I can't recall how we got there. But I do remember something Roy said. It has stayed with me all these years later. "You know, Terry," he said, slowly drawing his words out for effect, "You are only as sick as your secrets." Wow, was the first thought that went through my head.

He was right on.

After a few weeks, I did find a more permanent sponsor named John. He was a construction worker from Long Beach, and I was a city kid from Boston, so it was a marriage made in heaven, right? We had absolutely nothing in common. Four years later, he would be the best man at my wedding. In one of our first conversations John told me, "In the old days, my friends and I would sit on the wall at the beach, have a few beers, and solve the problems of the world."

I identified with John right away! My friends and I also thought we could solve the world's problems too over a few, well, let's say many beers, sitting on a wall at Cunningham park.

So, still stuck on step number four, I asked John what it meant by "a searching and fearless moral inventory?" He looked at me and said, "Terry, I would like you to write down all of the secrets that you have."

"Well I don't really have any secrets," I thought, "as everyone I have harmed in the past, knows about it, so it's not really a secret."

John thought that was hilarious. I guess he had never heard that line before, and then said; "So, for you Terry, I want you to start writing down the things you are not even going to tell God about."

"Oh, *those* secrets," I replied. And as crazy as that sounds, I had many secrets that I was not even going to tell God about. (Like God did not know them already.) I knew *exactly* what he was talking about.

So, over the next few weeks, I worked on my list of secrets, writing them down in great detail, starting with the ones I was not going to tell God about. I was very nervous. What if someone saw this list? What would they think of me? I decided in might be wise to keep these papers hidden. As for some people, this may be very hard to do. However, I now know that even if you are just willing to try this, that would be a very good start. Be willing to be willing, we used to say. You have to be willing to do this if you want to be *truly* free.

For years, it felt like I had an angel on one of my shoulders and the devil with black pitch fork and all, on the other shoulder. That little devil would often whisper in my ear things like, "Oh Terry, if other people knew 'that' about you, they would disown you. You never would have any real friends if they knew 'that' about you."

I now know that is a BIG LIE.

But that little devil on my other shoulder was no joke. He's crafty and, sadly, had been quite successful with me. I don't think most people think of Satan as a divider, however that is exactly his mission, to divide us with just about anything, especially other people. In fact, he is having quite a field day in this country and the rest of the world, right now. And he especially delights in separating us from our God.

You see, God (whoever that may be to you) really wants us to be truly and completely FREE. And I promise you, that if you will do this one simple exercise, you'll begin to feel that freedom that I am talking about. It'll be like a 50-pound weight being lifted off your back.

Frankly, it's one of the most amazing exercises I've ever done.

Here's how it happened for me. It took me about two weeks to finish off my list of secrets. Each day, I'd hide my work, as I thought that if anyone ever saw this, they would think I am crazy. When I had finished, I gave John a call and told him I'd completed my list.

He said, "Why don't we set up a time to talk? This Saturday, my wife and daughter will be out at one of her softball games, so no one else will be home, why not come over then?" So, I planned on going over to John's house that coming Saturday.

Now, one thing I've learned about these 12-step programs is the strong suggestion that when you share your 'list' to someone else, that men stick with men, and woman stick with other women. Sound advice I've learned. In addition, it is highly recommended that you NOT do this with your spouse. Not that you are hiding anything from each other, but this could be highly flammable 'stuff.' The bottom line is that it has to be someone that you trust completely. Of course, there are exceptions. Some women I know have shared their secrets with me as part of this process, largely because they felt they couldn't find another woman they could trust.

I understand that.

I do not really care, because you are not judging the other person, you are just listening to them get rid of their junk. The funny thing about me, is that I have a great memory, it's just short. Therefore, I could not tell you to this day what any one woman ever shared with me, nor would I, even if I could remember. That is not the point of the exercise. In addition, I never judge anyone who wants to truly get better and find freedom in this process.

By that Saturday I was a nervous wreck, the most anxious I think I've ever been—and I flew in jets for the U.S. Marine Corps, even landing on aircraft carriers at night when they looked like little postage stamps from the air. That said, I sucked it up and walked up his driveway and rang the doorbell.

I had no clue that my life was about to change—forever.

John answered the door. He's a big guy, about six feet four, and that might have been intimidating to my all of five feet ten inches, but John was one of the easiest going guys I'd ever met. I think it's one of the reasons we hit it off so well. Maybe it was just the laid-back nature of the folks who grow up in Southern California. He invited me in and offered me a soda. He had the Angels baseball game on. He kept it on, but turned the sound down just a little, so we could talk. I sat on the couch. He was in his favorite, well-worn chair. He looked at me for what seemed to be several minutes, but was actually just a moment. Then he said, "Whenever you are ready."

I felt like asking him about the Angels game, his childhood, how much he paid for the house, and where he got the cool chair—anything but the real reason I was there. I fidgeted—more like a squirm. I'm sure he could sense my discomfort. But he just sat there with a slight smile on his face, still trying to watch the game. He had clearly been in this situation before.

Good for him.

I started with a "hem" and "haw," searching for the right words while dancing around the issue.

"Do you have your list?" John asked.

I reached into my back pocket and pulled out some pieces of paper. I unfolded them and began to read my catalogue of secrets to him. After every few lines, I would look up at him, expecting to see shock on his face. But there was none. In fact, he was kind of passive, still with one eye on the Angels game. They were up to bat in the bottom of the fourth inning. At least I thought he was watching the game. When I finished reading the last of my sordid secrets to him, I remember feeling this tremendous sense of relief. I had done it!

I waited. More silence.

John was one cool cucumber.

"Is that it?" he said, finally breaking his silence. "Yep. That's all of them," I replied, confidently. "Oh, I've heard worse than that," he said.

Talk about a let-down. The secrets I shared were big deals to me. Major life blunders. Giant failures. Yet he seemed to minimize them.

"Okay," he continued, "now those secrets don't have any power over you anymore."

Simple as that.

What a statement! I truly had no idea about the *power* those secrets held over me for all those years. I thought I was a terrible person, or at least inferior to most people, but I wasn't. Finally, he said, "Now, I want you to burn that list. When you do that, you'll be ready for the next step, Terry." Again, simple.

All these secrets I had been carrying around for about 15 years, or so, things that were like an albatross around my neck, were gone. I wanted to bust out in a tune, that old *Chic* song, with Luther Vandross on vocals: *"Yowsah, Yowsah, Yowsah!,* but I didn't, still trying to hold my enthusiasm of what had just happened.

I learned a very important life lesson that day in John's living room, while the Angels were losing yet another game: Secrets are a *cancer* to the soul. And the longer you hide them, the more the cancer spreads. It metastasizes and destroys everything potentially good about you and your life. In fact, it reminded me of what Roy had told me earlier, *"You are only as sick as your secrets. Get rid of them ASAP!"*

I'm so blessed to have had someone to talk to about my secrets. My hope is that you can find someone to talk to, as well. If you can't think of anyone, why not try a pastor, or priest, or rabbi? By the way, Catholics, have a big advantage here, as they have the *Sacrament of Reconciliation or Confession.* As a postscript to this part of my story, several months after that breakthrough day at John's house, I heard that one of my favorite Hollywood actresses was doing a photo-spread for the December issue of *Playboy Magazine.* So, I bought my very first issue of Playboy. I found her pictures, but found myself feeling disappointed—at myself.

I threw the magazine away and immediately called John. I told him what I had just done. "I don't want any more secrets," I told myself. I don't need to be carrying that 50- pound pack on my back ever again! So, if I ever knowingly have a secret, I tell John or just about any of the men that I trust today, and who also trust me. Thank the Lord!

CHAPTER TWO
It's None of Your Business What Other People Think About You

"It matters little to me whether you or any human court passes judgment on me." – 1 Corinthians 4:3 (NAB)

Are you a people pleaser? Do you find yourself doing things to try to win the approval of others? Your parents? Your boss? Your teachers? If in the military, or other government official, your seniors?

For years and years, I never thought of myself, ever, as a people pleaser. I thought I was my own man and was not at all influenced by the opinions of others around me. After all, I was an aviator in the U.S. Marine Corps. I didn't have to please anyone.

Boy, was I wrong.

In fact, I lived almost half of my life trying to please other people. Where did that come from? It really does not matter. Could it be that I grew up with psychotic parents who were also alcoholics? For the life of me, I do not know. What I do know is that at one point in my life (when I was about 32) my world was crashing down upon me and I had a *big* problem that I had no idea how to handle.

So, I talked with my sponsor John, after a meeting one night in Laguna Beach, telling him that I had this huge problem and that I just could not figure things out. He looked at me and said, "Terry, I would like you to go home, say a small prayer, and write."

"Write what?

"Terry, go home, say a prayer, and write."

"John, you know I'll do anything you ask me to do that will help me improve my life, but what do I write about?"

He just looked at me and repeated, "Terry, go home, say a small prayer, and write."

Talk about not getting it.

But I decided to do what he said. I went home to my flat, said a small prayer, and put my pen to paper. My pen just took off, like it had a mind of its own. I must have written at least 15-20 pages, journaling if you will, about what was going on in my life at that time. It was all very exciting, but very painful, as well.

So, by doing this writing exercise, I was now able to identify my problem and immediately called John to tell him. When he picked up the phone, I said, "John, you're not going to believe this. I did what you told me and have about 20 pages of stuff to talk about, especially this problem I have. It's really big."

"That's great Terry," he said. "However, it's one o'clock in the morning, can we talk about it tomorrow?"

While frenetically writing, I had completely lost track of time. Now, I don't pretend to be a psychiatrist, but I knew I had this big issue to contend with, and I didn't know how to *fix* it.

Nowadays, for the life of me, and after all these years, I can't recall what the actual problem was, which is really funny to me. But I will never forget the principles John taught me, principles to be applied whenever a problem, big or small, arises.

John and I met the next morning at the *Laguna Hills Mall*. I joined him in his car. We were sitting just outside the *J.C. Penney's* on a beautiful sunny and mild Saturday morning. We had just been to a meeting and I was feeling my feelings, something new for me. Before this, I would just anesthetize myself with booze, woman, drugs, or a combination of all three. Whatever would take my mind off of the problem itself, whatever that may be. Now, I was going to meetings. I was journaling. I had other men in my life that I could trust. Up until that point in my life, I had never before had another man in my life that I could trust. It was just an incredible adventure on which I was embarking.

I told John about my problem. Unlike yours truly, he is a great listener. I went on and on for at least fifteen minutes before he looked at me in a way that made me pause. There was silence for a moment, then he told me to brace myself.

I did.

He told me that he had the solution for my problem. That is exactly what I needed to hear. **There is a solution**. Before this meeting with John and before he spoke that morning, I had always thought that there would never be a solution for any part of me. I was just a confused, messed up, guy. And now, here I was sitting on the edge of the car seat. John looked over at me and said, "Terry, it's none of your business what other people think about you."

I think I went into mild shock for a moment. I had no clue what he was talking about. So, I asked him to repeat what he said.

"It's none of *your* business what other people think about you!" he said, this time more emphatically.

I stared at him with what must have looked like a puzzled face. "It isn't?" I asked.

"No," he said. "People are going to think what they want to think about you and there is nothing you can do about it."

For a diehard people pleaser, like I was at the time, this was a revolutionary statement. I couldn't believe what I was hearing, yet, there was a part of me, deep down inside, that knew it was true. While I processed John's wisdom, he added a little postscript: He said, "Terry, 99 times out of 100, people aren't thinking about you, anyway. They're thinking about *themselves*."

Yet another illuminating pearl of wisdom from the mouth of John.

Therefore, my friends, if you are a people pleaser, like I was, try remembering that one simple statement: "It's none of your business what other people think about you." Try it for a few days or a week even. You'll experience the same kind of freedom I have been enjoying ever since that day in the Mall parking lot.

I was beginning to look at John like he was some sort of prophet. After these pearls, he looked at me and asked, "Terry, when was the last time you did something good for yourself?" Again, I had no idea what he was talking about. To be honest, I thought I was somewhat unworthy of doing anything just to please myself. So, I answered, simply, "I don't remember."

There was silence for a few moments, and then John said, "I want you to go out and do something nice for yourself. Be good to Terry today."

"Like what?"

"I can't tell you what. Buy yourself a nice shirt. Buy yourself a record." (Back then, there were such things.)

He was giving me permission to go out and do something nice for myself, and at that time in my life, I needed permission. So, when I got out of the car I walked into the mall and bought myself a nice new Hawaiian shirt, as well as a new *Santana* album.

I was so happy.

If you are a people pleaser, when was the last time you did something nice for *yourself*? If it has been awhile, or you can't actually remember any such occasion, I hereby give you permission to do just that.

Be good to yourself.

And remember, "It is none of your business what other people think about you. Ninety-nine times out of 100 people aren't thinking about you anyway. They are thinking about themselves."

And if you are really struggling with something, may I suggest that you go home, say a small prayer, and write.

But true freedom doesn't come without being tested—the proverbial trial by fire. My first test came just two weeks later. Some of the guys from my squadron used to go to a restaurant/bar in Laguna Beach appropriately called, *The White House,* just up the Pacific Coast Highway (PCH) from downtown.

Monday night used to be Reggae Night, and we would go dancing there, if you want to call it that. It was more like what Billy Crystal said in the movie, *When Harry Met Sally*, a bunch of white dudes doing what Crystal described as "the white man's overbite." It was hilarious, but fun, nonetheless. Naturally, the "brothers" would make us all look like fools. But then, I had just learned that it was none of my business about what other people think of me, and there was nothing I could do about it.

I drank *Coca-Cola* all night, however someone saw me and thought I had been drinking booze. He then went around town telling people that I was a fraud because he saw me drinking alcohol all night. So, I was a liar. Now, Laguna Beach is a relatively small town. People know each other, so that kind of gossip gets around pretty fast.

My first response was anger. But that lasted only about ten minutes. Then I remembered what John taught me: "It is none of your business what other people think about you, and there is nothing you can do about it."

In an instant, I was at peace.

CHAPTER THREE
Don't Die Wondering

"Don't die wondering, 'What if I could have done that… Die saying; 'I remember when I did…'"

– John R. Morris

I have done some pretty interesting things in my life. Some may even say I've done a lot of crazy things in the course of my life. My siblings used to call me Terrible Terence, but it was actually my older brother, Chas, who taught me most of the juvenile things I did. He is with the Lord now.

However, there are particular things that happened to me that taught me pearls of wisdom, and I feel an obligation to share them with others, realizing that we are all on different journeys in this life. This is one of those stories.

I was in the Marine Corps, and having completed my overseas tour, I was relaxing on a Saturday afternoon, while watching the Fighting Irish football team play some other team, and the Irish were cleaning their clock. During the break, a commercial came on television advertising the Big Brother, Big Sister program in Orange County, California. I thought to myself, "I have time to do that." So, I set out to be a big brother. It turned out to be a true blessing in my life.

When I started, I worked with one little guy, named Tony. He is a grown man now with a family of his own. Time really does fly. But back then, we would go surfing, bowling, or just hang out at the Camp Pendleton Marine Base. He really loved watching the soldiers marching, or climbing into old tanks, or even sitting in the cockpit of one of the planes I flew. It was a blast and I loved spending time with him. Many times, after a long day spent with Tony, I would go back to my flat in Laguna Beach and say to myself, "I think I had more fun than he did today." As I said, it was a true blessing.

After getting out of the Marine Corps, I took a job as a stockbroker. I noticed that one of the ladies at work, Barbara, was a single mom with a son about the same age as Tony. I asked Tony if it would be okay with him if we brought along another boy on our Saturday excursions. Very unselfishly, he said, "Sure."

So, we added Robert to our fun Saturdays.

One morning at work, this stunning, beautiful blonde bombshell walked into work. She walked up to Barbara, and talked to her for a few minutes, then she left. I immediately walked up to Barbara and asked her, "Who was that?!!" She laughed, and initially did not tell me, teasing me. After a few go arounds with her, I jokingly told her that I would not take Robert out again, unless she gave me details on this young lady. Finally, she told me that the young woman's name was Nina, and she was Barbara's au pair, from Finland. With impatience, I asked her, "Why have I not met her before in all of the times I have come to your house to pick up Robert?" Barbara told me that Saturdays were Nina's day off, so she was usually gone on the days that I spent with Robert. I insisted that I would have to meet her as soon as possible. She laughed and said that it would be a waste of time, as Nina had already been here for a year, and was leaving the following week to go back to Finland. Barbara then said, "Why don't you come over to the house tonight after work to meet her."

So, I did.

That night I asked Nina if she wanted to go down to Laguna Beach. I wanted to show her around. She said yes. We started out at the *Marine Room*, which is a bar, for a drink. We then went over to the *White House* to go dancing. After that, we got an ice cream and simply walked along the beach. I did not realize how late it had become, so I decided to head back to Barbara's house to drop Nina off.

On the drive back I told Nina that it was too bad that she would be leaving in a few days. She replied, "Well, why don't you come to Finland to visit me." I said, "Are you kidding me? Is Finland one of those Scandinavian countries? I will have to see." I pulled into the driveway to drop her off, and as I leaned in to give her a kiss, she looked at me with beautiful blue eyes, and said in her Finnish accent, "I don't want to go home yet." Well, I had that car in reverse and out of her driveway faster than a New York cab driver beeping his horn when the red light turns green in the city.

The next morning Nina again invited me to come to Finland and visit her. So I did. We spent ten wonderful days together, touring the cities and countryside before I headed back to LAX. The country was so beautiful and the people were so friendly, including Nina's parents. We had had a wonderful time. In fact, we had such a great time that I began to think of Nina as my girlfriend. She invited me to move to Finland to live with her.

Who, me? Move to Finland? A country that is joined at the hip with Russia? I had to think about that. We called each other numerous times over the next few weeks, which was not cheap. Remember, this was before cell phones and international calling plans. And over those weeks I realized that I was "in love" with her. I was a bachelor. I had no other prospects in the relationship department. All of my immediate family lived back in Boston. So, I decided, "What have I got to lose?" In all of my time in the military I had never traveled to Europe, so I thought, "Why not?"

I got my passport, got the details sorted out, packed up all my stuff (two whole boxes from my studio bachelor flat). I didn't own much back then. In addition, I could not afford to send my boxes by air, so I sent them by ship instead, which, I was told, would take roughly three weeks to get to Helsinki. (It ended up taking five weeks.) I then got a one-way ticket to Finland and was ready to go.

Two days before I was supposed to leave Nina called me and said, "Don't come." "What? Why?" I asked her. My belongings had already been shipped to Helsinki, I had my plane ticket in hand, and I was ready for my new adventure with the person I thought was the love of my life. When I asked her why she did not want me to come, she gave me some lame excuse about me not really knowing the language and that I would be hanging on her the entire time. (Translation: I later found out that she had gotten back together with her old boyfriend.) But, at that time, I did not know that.

I truly had a dilemma. I was about 31-years-old and did not know what to do. So, I went to one of my co-workers and friend, Howard, who was about 70-years-old, for advice. (He regularly gave me tips on how to look for stocks and how to buy those stocks.) He heard my dilemma and began to tell me a story.

Howard said, "When I was in college…." Now automatically, in my head I was thinking, "They had colleges back then?" He continued to tell me that in college he was dating a girl, but she had to leave school to take care of her mother, who was very ill. In my head, I was thinking, "What does this have to do with me and my problem." But I did not interrupt him, which was unusual for me.

He continued to tell me of the annual dance at the school. He had asked one of his girlfriend's friends to go to the dance with him. They went, had a good time, he walked her back to her dorm and never asked her out again. His original girlfriend missed two semesters of school, staying with her mother, until her mother died. When she came back to school, Howard told me he was afraid to ask her out again because he thought she was mad at him for taking her best friend to the dance while she was gone.

As he continued telling me this story, I continued to go crazy in my head because I so badly needed advice, and his story wasn't helping me….so far.

But then he turned to me and said, "What is the worst thing that could happen to you if you decide to go over there?" "Well," I thought, "the worst thing that could happen to me is that Nina would not want us to be together and things wouldn't work out. It would be a failure."

Howard concluded by telling me that he thought if he had asked his old girlfriend out again, they would eventually have been married. He went on to say that he truly believed his life would have been completely different if he had just asked his old girlfriend out again. But he never did. This wise, elder statesman then looked at me and said, "So then what would you do if you failed over there and things didn't work out?"

I answered, "Well, I would come back here to Laguna." He looked at me sternly, but very sincerely, and said, "Don't be like me. Don't die wondering."

After all that rambling, he had given me the answer. I did not want to die wondering whether or not I should have gone to Finland. So, I went. Nina still did not want anything to do with me. But I picked up a job at Citibank. The job was in an area called arbitrage trading, which these days is all done by computer, but it was so much fun trading millions of dollars in stocks every day.

While at this job, I was able to travel almost every weekend, to places like Sweden, Denmark, Russia several times, and even Israel. I saw such beautiful and historic places. What an adventure it turned out to be. I never would have been able to see all these places, especially not at the age of 31, if I had not listened to the best advice I have ever received in my life.

That one little tidbit was the best wisdom Howard could have given me, (aside from how to pick stocks). Things may have not worked out with Nina, but I learned a valuable lesson. To this day, I still live my life by this creed: I will never die wondering about anything in my life. I just do it, whatever *it* is, and it's been a grand life ever since that day.

In fact, just recently, I had asked a young lady, who is the manager of the chiropractic/physical therapy office that I go to, if she wanted to go out for lunch one afternoon. She has two small boys, and is a nugget. So, there was never any ulterior motive. Just a sandwich and conversation. My baby sister had just died and I felt like talking to a woman about her. Unfortunately, she dissed me and put on this big drama routine to boot. Whatever! One, I don't do drama, and two, I'm not going to die wondering if I should have asked her out to lunch or not. I asked her and now I know the answer. As they say down south, "That's how I roll."

CHAPTER FOUR
Patience/Humility

"Clothe yourself with humility towards one another."
— Peter 5:5 (NAB)

These two topics, patience and humility, have always eluded me and brought me both laughter and frustration. I freely confess that I am seriously behind the learning curve when it comes to understanding patience and being humble. How do I write about these vitally important, and so desperately needed human qualities?

I mentioned laughter. Here's a sidebar that fits that bill. When I joined the Marine Corps back in 1974, my recruiter gave me a bumper sticker that read, *"When You're the Finest, It's Hard to Be Humble,"* with the Marine Corps emblem of the eagle, globe, and anchor on it. It made sense to me back then.

It still does today. To me, there are few things in this world to be more feared than an 18-year-old young Marine with an M-16 rifle, or what we refer to as *real* Marines. Conversely, because I was a flyboy at the Marine Corps air base in El Toro, CA. (now Lake Forest and no base) we were commonly referred to as Hollywood Marines by the grunts in the Corps. Still the largest and best fraternity in the world.

Semper Fidelis brothers*!*

Anyway, admitting one's character defects, particularly in matters of patience and humility, for me is the beginning of wisdom. But I have been wired to see humility as a weakness. After all, I grew up in a household where we called my old man "The General," or as my brother and I used to call him; "General Nuisance." He had an ego the size of North America, and truly believed his excrement had no odor, if you get my drift.

Then again, he was the guy who dropped the second atomic bomb on Japan in August 1945—the one that destroyed the city of Nagasaki, and ended World War II. Heady stuff. But here's the thing—I never did, nor do I ever want to, be like him. If you've ever seen the movie, *The Great Santini*, with Robert Duvall, you have some idea what I'm talking about.

I wanted to be so much better of a person, than General Nuisance was, and I succeeded. And, as much as it goes against how I was raised, I know being that kind of person involves learning the grace of humility. In fact, it is one of the great needs in the world today.

Think about a few of your weaknesses. If you can't think of any, off hand—ask your spouse or closest friends. I'm sure they'll tell you. You see, personal growth and coming to the place of real freedom involves the on-going process of identifying weaknesses or flaws and then looking for effective remedies. Again, one of my most favorite lines, that both John and Roy instilled in me, was: **"There is a solution."** If I know there is a solution to my problem(s), then I know I'll be okay. And there is *always* a solution. Therefore, if you are not willing to look at your own shortcomings, and we all have shortcomings, then this would be an exercise in futility.

But as I said, I struggle with humility. Recently I told a friend of mine, a God-fearing man named Joe, that if someone opened a suitcase containing a million dollars in cash and told me that I could have it all IF I began to practice authentic humility from here on out, I'd have to pass.

That's not good, but it's true.

I really am trying to learn. Just this morning, during my prayer time, I came across a Catholic saint called *St. Humility*, the founder of a 13th century convent. Was it merely happenstance that I learned about her this morning, just as

I was trying to put this chapter together, about my personal struggle with pride? Frankly, I don't believe coincidences. It was definitely a "God Thing."

This wonderful woman, St Humility, was originally named Rosanna and was born in 1226 in Faenza, Italy to a very wealthy family. She was married at the age of fifteen and lost two babies who died as infants. Her husband, a man named Ugoletto, was nearly killed in 1250, and the event made him and his wife go through a time of personal examination. They eventually entered a monastery, where she took the name Sister Humility. She lived many years as a hermitess, and founded the convent of Santa Maria Novella on the island of Malta. She died in Florence in 1310.

She was the embodiment of humility in every way.

I have found that when I diligently and by faith seek answers to personal problems, answers have this way of popping up on my radar. And that's not just random chance—it's divine design.

I believe it was Nolan Ryan, after pitching one of his seven no-hitters, who was asked by a reporter about baseball players and their silly superstitions. He replied, "Superstitions are for people with weak faiths." Amen to that.

I must be honest with you. I know that both of these values—Patience and Humility—are vitally important. The problem is, as I mentioned earlier, I really do not know much about either one of them. I need your help. Could you help me finish this chapter? If you are willing to take the time to share your experiences, strengths and hope with these two subjects (not including smoking weed, taking valiums or Xanax), or anything like that, I will publish it either in my next book or on my blog. For those of you who have the wisdom, patience, and/or humility to help me, please take the time to go to my website www.terrysweeney.com, and tell us your pearls regarding these subjects. I, in turn, will then offer up that advice to others, in order to help others to get a handle on these two very important topics. So, if you have been blessed humility and/or patience please let me know. Simply go to the "contact" tab on my website and let us know. While there, check out the music tab as well…if you love music, as I do.

Thank you.

CHAPTER FIVE
You've Got to Give It Up to Keep It

"Whoever seeks to preserve his life will lose it, but whoever loses it will save it." – Luke 17:33 (NAB)

To me, this is the dichotomy of all dichotomies, the truest statement I know. What do I mean by *"you've got to give it up to keep it?"* What exactly do we have to give up? We use this saying often in the recovery world. However, it does not only apply to those in recovery. This saying simply means that we have to get out of ourselves and help others.

What do I mean by "get out of ourselves?" I've met a lot of people in my life that, in my opinion, can only be described as really self-centered. I call it the "ism": *I*, *Self*, and *Me*. I also think that most of these people tend to think about themselves about 90% - 95% of the time. Can you imagine what the world would be like if we reversed that into thinking about others, perhaps less fortunate than us, 90%-95 % of the time?

Social workers, nurses, and youth volunteers know exactly what I am talking about. Consider what is going on in our world today with this Chinese virus. Health professionals are our front-line heroes. They are literally risking their lives every day to help others.

What have you done lately to help another human being that is suffering? And I don't just mean financially, although helping someone financially is an incredible gift in and of itself. (In fact, 50% of all the proceeds of my books go towards charitable organizations). What I am talking about is someone who is struggling with a personal problem. With people who struggle with alcoholism, helping could mean driving them to a meeting, taking the time to listen to their tale of woe, or simply loving them until they learn how to love themselves.

Just four days before Christmas in the year 2000, a 27-year-old woman was distraught because she had just had a miscarriage. She was due in court with her landlord the next day because she owed $925 in back rent and had lost her job cleaning rooms at a local hotel. She was so distraught that she took her two daughters, ages five and seven, outside to the ninth floor of a building in Los Angeles and pushed them off, one at a time, to their deaths.

After watching them die, she then jumped, herself.

I heard this story on the radio on my way home from work that day. It received maybe a 20-second mention on the daily news. The next morning, I looked in the *Los Angeles Times* to see if there was anything written about it, but I found only a short story, in section B, on page 9. To me, there is something very wrong with this picture. On that same day in the *Times,* they were more concerned about runoff in the ocean that hadn't been filtered yet, and someone who broke his foot on a ride a Disneyland.

Those were the big headlines in the *Los Angeles Times* on December 22, 2000.

The young lady's name was LaShanda Crozier. Her daughters were Breanna and Joan. I mention their names here for one reason only. I ask that you stop now, wherever you are reading this book, and say a prayer, not necessarily for them, as I am confident that they are in *the land of milk and honey* now, but for those souls who are tempted by suicide every day.

Thank you.

In 2018, according to the CDC, there were 48,344 recorded suicides in the United States. That's up from 42,733 in 2014, according to the CDC's National Center for Health Statistics (NCHS). On average, adjusted for age, the annual

U.S. Suicide rate increased 24% between 1999 and 2014, from 10.5 to 13 suicides per 100,000 people. The highest rate recorded in 28 years.

Now I am going to ask you something even harder. Would you take the time to get out of yourself for a moment and think of a way that you could help the LaShandas of the world? There are plenty of people just like her, those who are suffering, struggling, and hurting—many of them right in your own neighborhoods. Would you take the time, talents and abilities that God has given you and offer them to someone who is in need? It doesn't have to be big. In fact, it may even be a simple, genuine smile.

I was prayed over on two occasions in what the Catholic church calls a deliverance. I'm guessing it something like an exorcism, but not nearly as intense, although this was very intense. Anyway, I remember this lady, Connie, praying over me, as I was laying prostrate on the floor, in the Chapel at her church, and not because I wanted to be in that position, it just happened that way. She demanded that the demon of suicide leave me. It took her three tries to get it out, and I will share this entire story in my memoir, however I did not even know there was a demon of suicide in me. It was incredibly powerful stuff, and not just that part.

So, for me, I do stuff like volunteering at a place that feeds the homeless a hot meal every night 365 days a year. We also have a trailer that has four showers that *our guests* can use every Wednesday morning. We also give away free underwear, socks, and undershirts etc., so when our guests are finished showering, they can at least put on new undergarments. What does that cost me? Well if I volunteer 3 days each week, at 4 hours per shift, that is 12 hours per week. That is so easy peasy to me, but even better is the reward I get from helping out. And I'm just one person. There are hundreds of volunteers who do this once a month, once a week, a few days each week like me, however it does not matter. My point is that you do have to give it up, your time, your talents and your treasures, etc. in order to keep them.

At the church I attend, we call it Mass plus one. What one thing are you going to do this week, aside from attending Sunday Mass that can help someone out in some way?

Back when my wife and I were newlyweds, we were living in Long Beach, CA, in a condo she had purchased. I would get up early to walk a few blocks to the gym for my morning workout. What seemed like every other day, I would pass by the same homeless heavyset woman, who was asleep at *her spot* on the sidewalk. I never knew her name, as she was always asleep when I walked by, but I did often wonder if there was any way I could help her. I really didn't think I could do much, to be honest. However, I decided if I did see her that day, I would slip a $5.00 bill into her pocket as I passed by. I knew in my heart of hearts that this lady would get so much more out of that $5.00 bill, than I would ever get out of it. Did she use that money to get a meal or a bottle? That's none of my business.

It helped her and it helped me.

In chapter three, I talked about how I became a big brother in the Big Brother/Big sister program in Orange County CA. For five or six years I 'worked' as a big brother for three different boys, two of which would eventually be ushers in my wedding, years later. And through all this service work, which consisted of four to six hours per week each Saturday, I was amazed at how much this helped me even more than it helped these young kids. We all had fun.

Trust me here, I am not perfect by any means. Just ask any one of my children. In addition, I am not trying to boast about the good Samaritan that I am. I am just giving some examples of what I do, or have done to get out of myself. I'm human and have probably wounded more people with my tongue alone, than I have helped others. But I have learned that helping others helps me to grow and change into a better person.

Perhaps you too can *give it up, to keep it.*

CHAPTER SIX
Acceptance

"If a person doesn't accept himself, it isn't rare that they don't accept others." – Humberto Del Castillo Drago

There is a saying out there that states: Acceptance is the key. "The key to what?" you might ask. I'm glad you asked. Let me tell you. Roughly 35 years ago, I met a man in Laguna Beach, CA. who became a good friend. We had many things in common. He went by the moniker, "Dr. Paul," as he was in fact a medical doctor. He had written an article in one of the 12-Step books I read.

Dr. Paul was quite a character, and he freely admitted that he used to prescribe any medication that he wanted for himself. I guess that is one of the privileges of being a doctor, unless you are an addict, which is what he had admitted to being.

Here is an excerpt from the article he wrote for the book:

Acceptance is the answer to all my problems today. When I am disturbed, it is because I find some person, place, thing or situation- some fact of my life- unacceptable to me, and I can find no serenity until I accept that person, place, thing or situation exactly the way it is supposed to be at that moment. Nothing, absolutely nothing happens in God's world by mistake. Unless I accept my life completely on life's terms, I cannot be happy. I need to concentrate not so much on what needs to be changed in the world as what needs to be changed in me and my attitude.

Do you need an attitude check? How about an acceptance check? I know I do on a regular basis. Sometimes daily, sometimes hourly, and sometimes minute by minute. So here is my challenge for you. Make a list of all the things in your life that are unacceptable to you. Once you have completed the list, find a small box, or perhaps an old shoe box, and put the list into the box.

On a second sheet of paper, make a list of all the things that you have and for which you are grateful for. You can start with your health, your eyes, your ears, your legs, etc. and move on from there. Once you have completed the second list, put it in that same box. (In reality these lists are never really completed.) There will always be more to be grateful for, as well as people, places and things that are unacceptable to you. Just keep putting them in that box.

On the outside of my box, I write the word G-O-D. If you do not believe in God, then you can name it something else. I label my box, God, and I refer to it as my God box. I have done this for quite some time now. I give all that "stuff" to God and get on with my life. Accept things as they are, focus on what you are grateful for, and let God take care of the rest. In fact, today I saw a funny bumper sticker on a car that read: *Man plans then God laughs.*

I always find it fun to, later down the road, go back and read the things that I have put in my God box as unacceptable. The problems that kept me up at night in the past. The things that got on my nerves. The things that I was angry at. Months later, I usually can barely remember them, and I can laugh at how they bothered me before I gave them to God.

If this exercise does not work for you, then you can do something else that I did when I was struggling with acceptance. I read the *Wall Street Journal* every day, which to me is the last bastion of neutrality in print. In my opinion, every other news outlet is either off the rails to the left, or too conservative to the right.

On December 28, 2019 I was reading the Saturday/Sunday weekend edition. On page A7, under a title called *World Watch*, there was a horrifying picture of about 100 little shanties that had caught fire in a slum in Bangladesh. The picture showed the people looking on, as their makeshift homes went up in smoke. I cut the picture out and it now hangs on my refrigerator door. I look at it four to five times every day when I am not on the road.

My friends, if you think your life sucks, ask the *Wall Street Journal* for a copy of that page. It will put things into perspective for you in a heartbeat. Compared to so many others, all over the world, we are blessed beyond belief.

It is truly unfathomable. Sincerely try, even if just for one day, to accept every person, place, thing, or situation exactly as it is at this moment. Then move on. If you do not have a smile on your face, then something's very wrong.

CHAPTER SEVEN
Heroes/Role Models

"Act as if your heroes are watching."
— Brother Anthony Freeman, LC

Do you have a hero or heroes in your life that you admire or wish to emulate? Most little boys growing up look up to a baseball or basketball player, while little girls look at their mothers as the person they most admire. My four daughters all had female *Disney* characters that they idolized. My oldest and most gorgeous daughter Eileen Grace is *Belle*, Maura, the most stunning redhead in the world, is *Cinderella*, newlywed, pregnant, and exquisite Siobhán (Irish: pronounced sha-VON) and means "The Lord is gracious," is *Sleeping Beauty*, and my youngest striking daughter, Maggie Pie is *Ariel*. In fact, my two married daughters, Eileen and Siobhán had their *Disney* characters as the themes for their weddings. Each was so cool. And, I heard the exact words a dad wants to hear from their daughters after their wedding, which is: "Dad, I had my day." That, my friends, is being the best parent you can be, for their biggest day.

I remember back in "the old days," I used to read the *Boston Globe* when I lived back in Boston, because I believe that it has, by far, the best sports pages in the world. While reading the sports page one week, I came across a number of different sports "heroes" in the news. Two were football players who were either in jail or in court for murder and rape. Below this, was an article on a basketball player who was charged with drunk driving. Another article told of a famous tennis player who was divorcing his wife and fighting for custody of his children—and his fortune. Finally, there was an article about a boxer who was subpoenaed into court for a palimony lawsuit.

All of this on the front page of the *Globe's* sports section that day.

Are these the role models and heroes that the youth of today are trying to emulate? If so, it is no wonder that we face some of the situations we do with our children today, the kind that parents just a generation ago never dreamed of facing. Are we putting too much emphasis on fame and celebrities or putting people who play professional sports on pedestals?

I've heard it said that we don't have heroes anymore, just celebrities. I will have to disagree with that statement.

One of my first heroes, or role models, is my former father-in-law. He is one of the few great men I have met in my life who still wants to learn and grow, even when I first met him in his sixties. And now, even in his eighties, he always wants to learn more! His thirst for information to grow emotionally and spiritually is unquenchable. He was also one of the first men that I ever met who admitted that he did not know all the answers, let alone all the questions. For men, this is a very rare trait, especially for older men, as they think they *know it all.*

Another hero of mine was introduced to me by my father-in-law. One afternoon, during a family gathering, he ushered me into his home office, with excitement in his Walter Matthau eyes. He handed me a book, written by a gentleman by the name of Og Mandino. It was titled, *The Greatest Salesman in the World.*

I loved this book, and I subsequently went out and bought all the other books that he had written. Each book is superb in its own right. Then, one day I heard that Og Mandino would be coming to Southern California to speak, and I knew I had to go and see him. What I did not know is that several of my friends were there too. I never knew that they were Og fans too. The talk was magnificent. Here was a guy who was homeless and wanted to kill himself. He was a hopeless drunk, who had put a gun to his head one night in total despair, hoping to end it all.

Have you ever felt that way? Just wanting to get away from it all? I know I have. But Og did not pull the trigger. I will not go into the story of his remarkable recovery. However, I can tell you he is worth reading about. Og died a few years back. However, he made a lasting impression on me, and hundreds of thousands like me. I think I have to add my former mother-in-law, Virginia, in there as well, because she tells me that she prays for me every day. I don't know about you; however, that is pretty special knowing that there is someone in this world praying for me every day!

I'm pretty confident that my spiritual director, Shirley Filadelphia, prays for me daily and lastly is Elle. I met Elle in Florida and was friends with her husband Ken, who recently died. She told me that she now prays for me every day. Three most beautiful woman. To me, that is pretty cool. Some of my children have even told me they pray for me every day as well. That's a lot of prayer being lifted up every day, just for this author.

These folks are just some of my heroes.

Do you have a hero(s) or role model(s) in your life? If not, I think you really need to get one or five. If you do have a hero or role model, ask yourself what is it about that person you most admire most. Then, on a daily basis, try to emulate some of those traits.

You will be amazed at the results.

Also, if you have the time, look up on whatever search engine you use, Mr. Laguna, Skipper Carrillo. Skipper has been the unofficial clubhouse manager of the baseball and football teams at Laguna Beach High School for decades. He turned 80 this year, and has not slowed down one bit. He remembers people by associating something, usually baseball names, about them with his heroes, that he remembers. For example, because I am from Boston, he refers to me as Ted Williams. He calls my friend Matt, The Duke. In addition, his mantra is always telling people to have a "home run day," whether helping the kids at the high school, or greeting them going into Sunday Mass at St. Catherine's of Siena Catholic church. Skipper had his own "home run day" on January 21, 2020, as the city of Laguna Beach elected to have a statue of Skipper made, and it was unveiled at the high school. Some people say that Skipper may be mentally challenged, however Skipper has never known hate in his life. So who has it right?

Skipper is also one of my heroes.

CHAPTER EIGHT
Are You the Best?

"Life is like a ladder. Every step we take is either up or down."

Are you the best at what you do? The best employee? The best parent? The best athlete? The best employer? The best dancer? The best artist? The best writer?

Back in the 1970s and 1980s, there was a UCLA college basketball coach by the name of John Wooden, otherwise known as "The Wizard of Westwood," who was, at the time, one of the winningest coaches in college basketball. One of my favorite quotes from him that he instilled in his players was, *"Never lie, never cheat, never steal."*

Can you imagine what our world would be like if just 50% of the population followed this simple rule?

Think about that for a moment. Never lie, cheat or steal. Coach Wooden went on to say, *"Nothing will work unless you do. Success comes from knowing that you did your best to become the best that you are capable of becoming."* He also said, *"Things turn out best for the people who make the best of the way things turn out."*

Coach Wooden had quite a few superstars on his teams as well throughout the years. One such star was Lew Alcindor (now known as Kareem Abdul Jabbar). Many people attribute the 1967-1968 "no dunking" rule to Alcindor. In fact, the no-dunking rule is sometimes referred to as the "Lew Alcindor rule." Another star was Bill Walton. Walton would constantly give Wooden a hard time, as Wooden chided him about his long hair, among other things. Yet Wooden turned him into a superstar, without taking any of Walton's baloney.

Wooden was not only famous for winning championship after championship. He was also famous because he taught these young men how to *live life* properly, even though they were already superstars. And just look at their lives today. If you are ever looking for a good read from John Wooden, I would highly recommend: *Pyramid of Success, The Essential Wooden, or A lifetime of Lessons on Leaders and Leadership.*

You will not be disappointed.

When I was a sophomore at Boston College High School, I ran on the track team. My favorite event was the mile. I was terrible at sprints and never had the stamina for a two-mile race. However, I loved the mile. I had a great kick and the mile was a perfect distance for me to pace myself and then kick at the end.

One day, our high school was at a track meet, competing against several other schools. We were a very competitive team, and I was one of the runners who was expected to earn points for our team that day by placing in one of the top three spots of my race. The race finally came and I ran my heart out that day, but unfortunately came in 6th place, not earning any points for the team. As I recall, if I had just scored points for our team, we would have won the meet that day. I felt like I had personally let the entire team down. Mind you, track and field events in those days consisted of 16 events in which teams could earn points, however I put the burden of the loss all on my shoulders.

It was a very quiet bus ride back to campus. It seemed that no one wanted to talk to me. I didn't want to talk to anyone either.

The next day at school, I barely raised my head while walking from one classroom to the other, looking down at my shoes most of the time. Then, in my geometry class, my teacher, and elder Jesuit priest, pulled me aside and asked me what was wrong. I looked at him quizzically and asked, "Haven't you heard the news? I was the one who blew it for our track team yesterday. I was the one that caused us to lose the big meet."

He looked at me and asked what I thought to be a very silly question. "Did you run your best?" "Of course I ran my best. I ran as fast as I could, I just didn't have it in me yesterday," I replied back. He looked at me sympathetically with his brown puppy dog eyes and said, "I'll be right back."

He came back to me with an anonymous quote, It says, *"Before God's footstool to confess a poor soul knelt, and bowed his head; 'I failed,' he wailed. But the Master said, 'Thou didst thy best—that is success!'"*

I did not realize that I had been successful at that track meet, because I had done my best. That is all I could do. I'm happy to say that I ended up winning the mile race at the next track meet. Oh, what a feeling!

So my friends, are you trying to do your best right now in whatever area of life that you are trying to succeed? Or are you just going with the flow, blending in, or trying to get by? What would your life be like if you just tried a little harder each day to do or be the best at what you do?

I did my best to instill this concept in my six children, as well, whether they were working at a fast food job, going to school, or playing sports. I told them if they ever got fired from a job, and if they had tried their best, they could hold their heads high, because they did the best that they were capable of doing. This also applies to school and life in general.

As the father of these beautiful children, and the sole breadwinner, because my wife was a stay-at-home mom who homeschooled our children, I was always able to be *there* for them. Was I perfect at it? Hardly. However, I do know that when my oldest daughter was eight-years-old, she asked me if I would take her out dancing, or my oldest son, Grady, when he was six-years-old, had the courage to tell me that I hurt his feelings earlier that day because I had yelled at him. I must have been doing something right as a dad. Trust me, when I was six years old, I would never have had the courage to tell my father that he had hurt my feelings. I would have ended up across the room, with the hit he would have given me.

I mentioned earlier that I didn't even know what feelings were until I was about 30. My brother-in-law Brian (call sign, Bear) was flying A-4's for the Marine Corps in Vietnam when I signed up to join the Marines to learn how to fly. In a way, I wanted to be just like him—not some pansy Air Force guy like my old man. Brian gave me some great gouge. Gouge in the military means information, as in: Who has the gouge on what we are doing today?

He told me that if I was in top physical shape when I went to boot camp (which you had better be, or you're a fool),

80% of boot camp will be mental. He was exactly right. The drill instructors will mess with your mind all night and day long. There is nothing wrong with that, as the Marine Corps is the only military branch of service, that I know of, that tells you as soon as you get off the bus/cattle car that you will be a trained *killer*. And they will mess with your head just to see if you had the gonads to do what they told you to do. It was all about breaking you down, and building you back up their way. A brilliant way of training success.

I do not remember too many guys getting dropped because of the mental anguish. You just had to be tough both mentally and physically. So, if you do the very best you can, and still get dropped, you can hold your head high, as you did your very best. That is success. The Marine Corps is not for everyone. That is why they have the most intense boot camps of all the services.

Harder than Marine boot camp is Navy *Seals* boot camp. By far the toughest training in the world, both mentally and physically, however they give candidates/trainees a cop out. After all, less than 20% of all trainees ever make it as *Seals* anyway. However, if you want to *volunteer out*, you go to the bell that sits in the middle of the beach and ring it 3 times. The sound sends a deafening echo throughout the training camp, letting everyone know that you have one more quitter. Naturally, the Navy *Seals* are not for everyone either, however, I never liked the thought of that bell. If you do not make it and get dropped, you can still hold your head high, as you gave it your best. If you ring the bell, you are looked at as a quitter.

Don't ring the bell in your life. Be the best you can be… period.

CHAPTER NINE
Pornography

"Each man must look within himself to see whether she who was entrusted to him as a sister in humanity…has not become in his heart an object of adultery."
— St. John Paul II

Here's a fiery topic. However, I'm just trying my best to be obedient, that's all. Actually, there are some very salient points in this chapter, should you decide not to skip over it.

I recently read an article that claimed that 80% of adolescents aged twelve - eighteen had already viewed some type of Internet pornography. I immediately felt sick. And this is worldwide, not just in the United States. So, if I understand this correctly, there is a very good chance that young girls and young boys have already viewed intercourse on-line. If that is true, and the innocence of these children has been taken away so early in life, society as a whole is in trouble.

Pornography has become a gigantic problem in our world today. We are constantly bombarded with graphic images from billboards, television, cable shows, movies, and the internet. Today pornography and sexual imagery are ubiquitous and widely available. And we are constantly being sold on the idea of sex and the pleasure it brings us.

In fact, in a 2015 study done by Tom Jacobs of the *Pacific Standard*, wrote in an article titled, *Pornography Consumption on the Rise*, that as the internet grew, so did the proliferation of pornography. They fueled each other. His study also found that there was a large increase in the viewing of pornography, due to access to the Internet. Finally, he found that the largest viewing increase occurred between people born in the 1970s and the 1980s. Mr. Jacobs noted that children born in the 1980s forward, were the first generation to grow up in a world where they had access to the Internet beginning in their teenage years. And this early exposure and access to Internet pornography may be the primary driver.

Most people do not realize that by viewing pornography, a person (male or female) learns to measure the value of the of the other man/woman based on how much lust they have for that person. People also do not realize how their ability to love is being crippled. If the use of pornography continues, lust will then seem natural. Then when you try to love another from the opposite sex, or even the same sex, if you are gay, you'll find yourself confused and disappointed.

Oh, then there is always the argument, "What? I'm not hurting anybody." What about your wife, husband, girlfriend, boyfriend, daughter, son, or the men and women who are in the porn industry? Do you think they lead a normal life? Do you think they are not being exploited? What if that was your child? After all, they all have parents.

It has been proven that pornography trains a person to get bored with commitment. So ladies, have you ever wondered why that guy you are living with and are giving free milk to, will not/has not made a commitment to you? Or vice/versa guys? Now you know the answer.

Not surprisingly, additional research on people who view porn, found that **they were less likely to be satisfied with their partner's affection, physical appearance, sexual curiosity, and sexual performance**. This behavior then has led them away from what they were seeking in the first place. In the words of one husband: "The best way to ruin pleasure is to make it your goal."

If God has created us to love as He loves, it is no wonder that those who view porn are never satisfied. The fact that strip clubs refer to themselves as "adult" entertainment and "gentlemen's" clubs proves that no matter how far men fall, they still feel a need to identify with authentic manhood. Why?

A famous Catholic saint, Alphonsus Liguori, once noted that when a raven finds a dead body, its first act is to pluck out the eyes. Similarly, for those addicted to pornography their eyes/light is taken away. I do not think I am telling you anything that you do not already know.

Many years ago, I had a great conversation with a good friend of mine about the subject of pornography. I asked him if he ever struggled with the issue. He admitted that he had. He said he wished there was no pornography in the world and that all of the companies that produced it would go out of business. He said to me, "If we did not buy it, they would all go out of business." He stopped buying it. But unfortunately, one person stopping buying it does not put a dent on the industry as a whole. And now with the internet, people do not have to spend money anymore. All you have to do is type in a porn sites address on the Internet and you will be blasted with filth from the first page. That's it. In your face.

And it's all free!

Another dear friend of mine, who has one of those old Obama-phones, was showing me her phone one day and how antiquated it was. She had earlier told me that she uses her phone to view porn. "Everyone does," she stated to me matter-of-factly. She's young, yet has one of the most beautiful hearts of anyone I've ever met in my life. However, I felt it was my job to let her know that her statement just wasn't true. That was a tough one, because she is so sweet, but I did it. I then offered to get her a new cell phone, if she wanted one, however she could not look at porn on the new phone. She elected to keep her old Obama-phone. That was a very powerful statement to me as to just how dominant/influential this really is.

Recently, I was having a conversation about the issue of pornography with a close friend, Father Tim, who is also a Catholic priest. He said to me, "Terry, this is not only a problem for men, but for women as well…and not just young women, but older women, too." I was shocked at that statement. However, with the ease of access to pornography, without cost anymore, I don't know why I was so surprised. I told him that I have had, over the years, friends, both male and female, admit to me that they are addicted to pornography. I asked Father Tim if had any advice that I could pass down to those addicted to porn.

He gave me these suggestions. First, one must realize that he or she is not alone in the struggle. Second, pornography addiction needs to be treated like any other addictive behavior––e.g., alcoholism, drug addiction, smoking, and food addiction. Third, if someone is struggling with pornography, that person must realize that he or she is powerless over it. Fourth, he/she must understand that addiction is a disease, and not necessarily a moral failure. Fifth, if someone is trying to recover from pornography addiction, he/she must be patient with themselves on the journey, remembering that the problem did not begin overnight and it will not end overnight.

Lastly, you can pray every day and ask our Lord to help give you the grace each day to avoid this addiction. As with all 12-step programs, we can only do it one day at a time. Peace.

[Author Note: I am indebted for the wonderful website: www.chastity.com for material used in this chapter – TS]

CHAPTER TEN
Anger

"Who does not persist in anger forever, but delights rather in clemency." — Micah 7:18 (NAB)

Anger is a subject with which I, unfortunately, am very familiar. However, as I continue to grow and learn about becoming the best version of myself that I can, layers of the onion, or myself—my character defects and flaws—are exposed and then peeled away. It is not uncommon to not like what you see in yourself when peeling that onion. However, if you truly want to be set free, you have to do the work.

My issues with anger were one of the main character defects I carried around for a long, long time. Many of us do. If you don't think you have a problem with anger, or if you are in denial, a good exercise is to ask a trusted friend, family member or spouse, if they see any anger signs with you. If they say yes, then trust them and admit that you have this shortcoming as well.

Before I acknowledged that I had a drinking problem at the age of 30, everyone around me—my family, friends, neighbors, and co-workers—all knew I had a problem with alcohol. But I couldn't admit it myself. I was definitely in a state of denial.

It was the same with my anger issues.

For years, those closest to me told me that I had anger issues. But I would always blame my anger on a situation, a particular circumstance, person, or event. I had been wronged. I blamed others. Why couldn't people understand that? If they had experienced what I had, they would have been angry, too! I couldn't see the truth until things finally came to a head in the mid 1990s.

I was 41-years-old.

I had taken a job with a healthcare company in Klamath Falls, Oregon, because I thought the proverbial grass was greener there. It is greener, because it rains so much in Oregon. I believed this move was a way to escape the rat race I was experiencing while living in Southern California. When I interviewed for the job, there was a horrible, snow storm going on. I could only see a few feet in front of me for the two days that I was there. We called these *white-outs* in Boston. Quite a difference from Southern California. My wife, who was a native of Southern California, had never seen a white out nor even heard the term. So, when I when I got back from my interview, she asked me about the town. I told her there was a white-out the entire time I was there. "Yes, but what does the town look like," she replied. So, I explained to her what a white-out was. That way, we both would be surprised at what we found on our journey to Klamath Falls, Oregon.

So, we moved from Southern California to occasionally gray and rainy Oregon. We bought a simple house that had a bay window overlooking California's Mount Shasta. It was a very picturesque setting. For the first year in my life in Klamath, I felt that everything seemed to go very well on the new job, as well as at home. My wife became pregnant with our third child, Siobhán Kate. She was so beautiful. She still is! The two other children were enjoying the change of scenery and my wife seemed to be able to relax a little bit more.

However, after a year or so, events and personalities were starting to get to me….as usual. People just didn't *get* me. To me, Klamath Falls seemed to be stuck in some old ways. It was an old potato farming place. There are no actual *falls*, in Klamath Falls. People did not accept any type of change. In fact, at one point, someone suggested to the city council to put in some flowers and greenery in between the main roads to spruce up the town, as many cities across America do. But the suggestion was quickly turned down.

Weird.

Well, one day, while I was driving back from a sales appointment in Bend, I found myself in a bit of a predicament. The highway department had been repaving the road and only had one lane open for both lanes of traffic. I could see that the traffic worker was waving cars through on my side. I sped up so I could get directly behind the last car being waved through. If I did not make it through, I would have had to wait another twenty minutes before they opened up my lane again. I wanted to get home to play with my little ones. The highway worker saw me speeding up and, just as I was about to pass through, he put out his stop sign. Just for my car. There were no other cars behind me.

I put down my window and said, "Come on man. It's just one car." He looked at me sternly and said, "I said stop." He had to be all of 19-years-old, and was obviously on a power trip, getting his jollies at my expense. He had the power to stop my car.

I put the window up, ignoring him and proceeded to follow the car in front of me. The next thing I knew, I heard yelling. He was yelling to his coworkers, "That car hit me! That car hit me!" It was then that I saw several highway workers with hot iron rakes of tar coming toward my car.

Not knowing what to do, and panicking, I drove onto the portion of the highway that they had just paved and barreled down the road for about a quarter mile, digging up everything that they had just finished doing. What a nightmare! At that point I was just in a hurry to get home.

About ten minutes later, I was pulled over by the state police.

Thankfully, when I told the trooper what had really happened, he did not give me a ticket. However, I first had to go with him back to the scene. It was obvious then, that I never came close to hitting this kid with my car. Then, I gave the police officer all of my information, just in case the state elected to seek damages. When I got home that evening, I told my wife that we were going to have to find another place to live. I just couldn't take it any longer. In my mind, the whole situation was not my fault. Everyone else was to blame, this time this young kid.

The very next day, as I was looking through my employee benefits package, I noticed that they offered free counseling for employees, through a program called *Employers Assistance Program* (EAP). Many companies in the United States have these programs, and we were no exception.

If the option at your workplace is there, I highly recommend taking advantage of these programs, as they are no cost to the employee seeking assistance. And everything is held in strict confidence.

I decided to take advantage of the opportunity and made an appointment to see one of the counselors. I wanted to find out why I was so frustrated all the time. I told him about all of the personality conflicts I experienced at work. I mentioned all the annoyances I dealt with at home. Finally, I told him about my little "incident" while driving the day before. The counselor looked at me with a big smile on his face. He told me that he knew why the highway worker was stopping my car but not the others.

"Why?" I asked impatiently. Looking at me intently, he said, "Because he didn't know who you were." I was not amused. He then went on to say, "You see, if you had had a sign on the front of your car that said *Terry Sweeney*, then he would have let you pass through. But he didn't know. He didn't know that you had been a pilot in the Marine Corps or that your wife was pregnant. You see, if he had known all that, of course he would have let you through. He just did not know." I could see the point that he was trying to make, however I was both boiling mad that he had pointed this out to me and laughing on the inside as well. He was implying that I thought that the world revolved around me and I got angry anytime that people didn't recognize that.

He was right of course. Just like my old man, I said I would not emulate.

The counselor looked at me warily and then told me that he had been teaching anger management classes for men for over the past 15 years. Then he said, "Terry, you have anger issues. If you are willing to admit that, I will be happy to work with you one on one. I think I can help you."

What a blessing that was. I ended up getting 100 hours of community service because of my little "incident" on Oregon State Highway 97. I never really did my service hours, but that's another story.

The anger management counseling helped me tremendously, although I still had anger relapses periodically.

Years later, one such incident occurred. My oldest son asked me if he could have his buddy over for a sleepover, which was not a problem. I am one of those parents who preferred that my children have people over to our house, rather than them going to someone else's house for the night.

The boys asked me if I could take them to *Blockbuster Video*. They rented two movies, using their own money. And that was that. The next morning, my son asked me if I could drive his friend home, with another stop at *Blockbuster* along the way. Again, this was not a problem. We drove to the video store, where my son dropped the two movies into the overnight drop box, as they had not opened yet.

About a week later, my son got a call from *Blockbuster* stating that he had never returned the movies he had rented. I went ballistic! After all, I was with them when they rented the movies, and I was with them when they dropped off the movies the following morning.

I called the store and told them what had happened. They said that they did not care about my side of the story, and that they were going to have to charge my son for the two movies. So, I asked my son to come with me down to *Blockbuster*. We went in, and I told him to pick out the two movies he had rented. My thought was that if they were going to charge him for these movies, then he should be allowed to actually possess the movies. He did what I asked him to do. As we were walking out the manager started chasing us out of the store. In her haste, she pushed the door so hard that the glass door shattered.

Sweet revenge! I thought to myself.

Another man came running out to the parking lot, acting like he wanted to fight me. I ignored him, but he kept coming toward me. So I said to my son, "Hold these movies." He took the movies, and I started walking toward the guy. I was prepared to knock his lights out. He ran away. I guess he wasn't so tough, after all.

The employees at *Blockbuster* called the police. The police then came to our house about an hour later. My wife absolutely freaked out. I think she thought they were going to take me to jail. I knew better, having been in trouble with the law since I was 14. But the police simply asked for the movies back and then left. It was kind of anti-climactic. Unfortunately, my son had to pay for the movies he never received. Ultimately my anger issues came back up that day because I never want anyone to intentionally hurt my children. In the heat of the moment, I had forgotten some of the things I had learned from that counselor in Klamath Falls.

Knowing that I had a problem with anger early on is not the same as working on the problem. I learned this about alcoholism. Admitting that I had a problem was only half the solution. The other half is to actively work through the issues that are causing the problem in the first place. My outside anger was just a symptom of the *inside* problem.

Unfortunately, we are not necessarily "cured" from our character defects, but we can get help for them and ultimately learn to be better people, despite our shortcomings, and we all have shortcomings.

What character defects do you struggle with? What have you been told by others that you may be in denial about? If you are struggling with the answer to these questions, write down your thoughts. Discuss your thoughts with a friend, and ask them what they think.

If you believe you have a problem, then look for ways to get help in those areas. If your company has an EAP program, by all means use it. Help is available. You just have to reach out and ask for it. However, the first thing you must do, is admit to yourself that you have this problem, whatever that problem may be. The end result, my friends, is a more peaceful and happier life.

If you would like to go to our website at www.terrysweeney.com and voice your opinion of this topic, we would love to hear from you.

CHAPTER ELEVEN
Prejudice

"This is the second: You shall love your neighbor as yourself. There is no other commandment greater than these." – Mark 12:31

If you would, please take a moment to ask yourself if you are prone to pre-judging others. That is what prejudice is. It is pre-judging of others. If you answered no to that question, I would encourage you to really think about it. Go back and reread the statement. If you still say no, then maybe you are one of the rare human beings that have no prejudice towards others. But I would venture to say that most of us are prejudiced to some degree or other, whether it is directed towards race, gender, sexual orientation, income level, level of education, etc. We treat people differently based on a number of things. One example,

I know of, is an elderly lady in Los Alamitos, CA. who cannot stand Asian drivers and how slow they drive. That's funny to me, but she's right.

I was raised in a racially prejudiced home. In addition, I am not here to bash my parents, or anyone else for that matter. I am simply stating a fact and trying to be honest. After all, no one has ever actually *seen* a motive.

I grew up in a suburb south of Boston. At that time, busing, race riots, and the Vietnam war were all very big issues. Unfortunately, I was caught up in the bigotry of the time. It wasn't until I moved out of Boston, out of that toxic environment, and grew up that I realized how truly sick I was when it came to the issue of race.

I finally saw how much of a prejudiced person I had been when I began to change around the same time I elected to stop drinking alcohol. It was only when my ego started to deflate, and I began to see myself for who I really was, that I began to understand that we are all God's creatures. Throughout history, our forefathers, respected Presidents, and men like Dr. Martin Luther King Jr. preached this message all the time.

When I finally took a good hard look at myself it really was not that hard for me to take the first step and admit that prejudice was an issue for me. So for me, I set out to change the way I viewed others and treated those different from me. First, I stopped telling and listening to racist or ethnic jokes.

As I grew closer to God, I looked to Jesus for an example. It was very hard for me to imagine Jesus sitting around a campfire with His disciples telling *Gentile* jokes.

Second, I changed the language that came out of my mouth. I no longer use certain derogatory and hurtful words that I constantly heard from my mother and siblings as I was growing up. Never from my dad, by the way. He would just see a very heavy set woman and say to me things like, "Now there's a girl that loves her vegetables." Or, "What's wrong with big girls. They give you shade in the summer and keep you warm in the winter." Dad ism's. My children never heard me speak this way. We call that breaking the chain.

Finally, I try to go out of my way to intentionally treat with kindness the people that I used to dislike because of the way they looked. Changing these "little" things has had a big impact on the man I am today. I am a much better person today. My children have never heard a derogatory word from me about any other ethnic race, creed, or color. I have lived in many different places around the world and today I have friends of every race, creed, and color.

As I said earlier, my friends and I call this type of change *breaking the chain*. Courageous people, who really do want to grow and better themselves are breaking the chain of alcoholism, prejudices, denial, etc. every day! Thank God.

By the way, in 2020 we are hearing a lot of the term systemic racism. I do not believe it one bit. You simply cannot live in a country that not only elected the first black President, then re-elected him again, and then say we have a systemic race problem. Do I believe there is still racial inequality? I know there is. But to say that is America is systemically racist is a bunch of BS to me, and just another way these radicals are trying to tear our beautiful country apart.

Satan, the great divider, is having a field day. Don't fall into his trap!

CHAPTER TWELVE
Ego

"A man wrapped up in himself makes a very small bundle." – Benjamin Franklin

Ego. The word itself sounds like some type of bug that one would find in the forest. What exactly is an ego? Who has an ego? How do we get an ego?

Webster's Dictionary defines the word, ego, as:

1. An exaggerated sense of self-importance; conceit;
2. Appropriate pride in oneself; self-esteem.

The English word "ego" is the Latin word for "I." So, if you were to write "I love you" in Latin, it would be *ego amo te*. The use of the term as a synonym for pride was popularized largely through the work of Sigmund Freud.

In twelve step programs, we have our own slightly different perspective about what Ego is. We describe it using an acronym: ***Edging God Out***. I love this definition because when our egos become too big, that's exactly what we are doing. We are edging God out of our lives, maybe because of pride, self-centeredness, and/or self-reliance.

When our egos are running the show, we feel that we are in control. When we have climbed to the top, when we have made the big sale, when we have won an argument, we think, "I did it!" Me, myself and I.

I have a dear friend named Paul. He lives in Boston. He dated one of my younger sisters for a while, and we played High School football together. He was the star running back, and I played the positions of guard, tackle and end. In other words, I sat at the *end* of the bench, *guarded* the water bucket, and *tackled* anyone that went near it. I will never forget the great times we both had in high school.

When I got married, Paul flew out from Boston to be at my wedding. Years later, when he was getting married, I flew back to Boston to attend his wedding. He was one of the last of our high school "crew" to get married, and all of the old gang was there.

At my table at the reception was another one of our old cronies—Jack. He had had gotten married two years before Paul and now had his own little bundle of joy. I had two children by this time, and I said to him, jokingly, "We sure have come a long way from drinking beer down at the park, to changing poopy diapers."

He gave me a strange look and said very seriously, "I don't change diapers. That is my wife's job."

I almost didn't believe him. So I asked him, "Are you telling me that you have never changed a diaper in your life?"

"Absolutely not," he replied. "Nor will I ever."

"Wow," I thought to myself. "How selfish and self-centered is he!" His ego had gotten the best of him. Perhaps he was trying to prove to the "boys" that he was still a tough guy, as we all thought we were, back in our teenage days.

But I have since learned that there can be no ego in my life. My wife and I were blessed with six beautiful children. We viewed our marriage as a team effort, not an individual ego fest. I cannot even tell you how many diapers we each have changed over the years, but I never looked at that as a chore. It was more of a duty.

I did not pursue the conversation any further with Jack, because I knew him too well and it would not have done any good. I kind of felt sad for him. Not that changing a really stinky diaper at 5:00 a.m. is ever fun. But where is it written that this task is only performed by women? What kind of partnership did he have in his marriage? Does he have an actual partnership, or does he just have a big ego problem?

Another example of ego came to me one day while I was at the dentist. Before my appointment, I usually use my *Waterpik* and then my electric toothbrush, to at least look like I was making an effort to keep my teeth clean. And to protect the hygienist from anything gross.

The hygienist told me a story about when she used to work on the rich side of town. It was a normal thing for the men to come into the office after having lunch without any effort to clean their teeth before a cleaning. When the hygienist asked her patient one day why that was, the man replied, "I'm here so that you will clean my teeth, and I want to get my money's worth."

I don't know about you, but that just strikes me as wrong. Ego puts self over others.

God wants us to put others first.

Remember, ego is *edging God out*. Are you edging God out of your life? Take a moment to reflect on how you treat others. Are you self-centered and selfish? If nothing comes to mind, then sit down, say a small prayer, and write.

After all, if you think you are perfect, that might just be your ego.

CHAPTER THIRTEEN
Peace

"Then the peace of God that surpasses all understanding will guard your hearts and minds in Christ Jesus."
— Philippians 4:7 (NAB)

I grew up in the 1960s, which Charles Fleischer claimed; *"If you remember the 1960s, you weren't there."* I try not to remember much about the 60s, as a lot of it was very painful for me and the other part was a lot of fun. We did not have ANY restrictions, as kids do today. We went anywhere and did whatever we wanted to, anytime we wanted to. But if you were not home when the cow bell on the back porch rang out at 6:00 pm for dinner you simply didn't eat supper, period. 10 kids and 2 parents at dinner every night. What a debacle! But my mom or older sisters pulled it off every night. Truly amazing!

I do however, distinctly remember the rock concert in upstate NY, called Woodstock, because my older brother, handsome Chas, went to it. I was so mad that I wasn't old enough to go. But, like my brother, when I was a teenager, in the early 1970s, I remember experimenting mostly with drugs and alcohol, too.

And I remember that the word *peace* was a big deal.

The Vietnam War was going in full swing in those days. Richard Nixon had followed Lyndon Johnson as President of the United States, and for the first time in history the images of war could be seen each night on the television news. In fact, the conflict in Vietnam became known as "The Living-Room War." It was really ugly, to watch *real war* on television, as all wars are really ugly.

But people longed for peace. It was insane to watch a live war at home, while knowing that family members were over there.

Sometimes we rioted in Harvard Square in an ironic attempt to bring it about, similar to what we see going on in our country today.

We had peace symbols, and bought tie-dye shirts with Churchill's "V for Victory" sign from a generation earlier had been transformed into the peace sign. We read books about peace at school. Song lyrics written by John Lennon asked us to give peace a chance.

Now, here we are 50 years later and it seems like history is repeating itself. The news is again filled with rioting and many are begging for peace. People who feel they have been wronged protest in a fight for peace. The "fight" for peace was an oxymoron that I had a hard time understanding as a child, and I still do today.

Isn't peace, by definition, the opposite of fighting?

My dad was a two-star general in the Massachusetts Air National Guard. When I was in high school, I remember him saying to me one morning on the way to school, "Terry, the United States has never been at peace for more than twenty years." I have never forgotten that statement from him. It will always resonate with me. He was right of course.

Naturally, I had to fact check the old man's claim, and I found out that he was absolutely right. The *military industrial complex* that President Eisenhower warned us about in his 1961 Farewell Address is alive and well in the United States and around the world. The military industry is a big, big business, so we shouldn't be surprised. Think about the building of a military jet. Every separate piece of equipment and accessory, down to the pilot's helmet has to be crafted. Production provides countless jobs to employees in every congressional district across the country.

There was a great spy picture that came out in 1990 called, *The Russia House*. It starred many famous actors, including Sean Connery, Michelle Pfeiffer, Roy Scheider, John Mahoney, and James Fox. It is one of my favorite movies, and it gives a great example of how the military industrial complex works. I also love this picture, because I was in Russia a lot, when I lived in Helsinki, with the little matchbox cars and the poor simple life of most Russians at that time. Their motto is, "The government pretends to pay us, and we pretend to work." I do know that the everyday Russian people treated me more kindly as any country I've ever been in, with the exception, maybe, of South Koreans, who absolutely love Americans. These folks would invite you into their two-room apartments, because that's all you get are two rooms, and a tiny kitchen. They would make us tea, and would take the shirt of their back, if you needed a shirt. Just super nice people. As Sean Connery says in that movie, "The poor bastards just want to be like us." How true. In fact, in my opinion, if things get really out of hand, Russia would be one of our allies. I hope things don't get out of hand.

Throughout history, we have constantly searched for peace in the world around us. But I believe that if we are ever to find peace in the world, it has to start *within* us. We must look inside ourselves first.

How do we do this? First, we have to remember not to beat ourselves up if we make a mistake or don't do something perfectly, or for taking a risk and failing. And we should try to stay calm and peaceful no matter what is going on around us.

I do not curse the guy who just cut me off in traffic anymore. I do not yell at my children anymore. It has to start with me and works best from the inside out.

If I can somehow learn to be at peace with myself, I may be able to pass it on to others. And if enough people do this, then maybe it will change the world. With regard to the outside world, I am helpless and powerless over what other people, groups, and nations do. Current events around the world, and the devastating things we see on the news here at home, are out of my control. The only thing I can control is my reaction to whatever comes my way. I did my part for my country, serving as a Marine Corps aviator, both in active duty and the reserves. I did the job I was asked to do, which involved reconnaissance, the taking of pictures of various locations around the world, as we were ordered to do. So to those who say, "Thank you for your service," I say, "Thank you for your support."

The other thing I can do for peace is pray. One of my first Bible class instructors was a lady by the name of Josie, at St. Kilian's in Mission Viejo. I remember her stating that; "The evil one would like you to believe that there is nothing you can do about world situations, so why even bother? However," she continued, "I stand here today to tell you that that little old lady crossing the street and praying to God for peace is a more powerful force than any country's military."

She was so full of wisdom.

So each day I pray for myself, for my loved ones, both living and deceased, and for those who have asked me to pray for them. And I pray for peace.

Where in your life do you lack peace? It has to start from within. Write it down on a piece of paper. Try to find a quiet spot in your home to go to, maybe even light a candle and start praying for yourself and for peace. That may entail starting with your own hearts.

CHAPTER FOURTEEN
Forgiveness

"Be kind to one another, tender-hearted, forgiving each other, just as God in Christ also has forgiven you."
– Ephesians 4:32 (NAB)

The Bible has a lot to say about forgiveness. In fact, most religious institutions teach this important principle. One verse that has always made me think of forgiveness is the second greatest commandment given in the Old Testament Book of Leviticus and reiterated by Jesus. It's found in Mark 12:31, which says, *"You shall love your neighbor as yourself."*

When I was young I had a very hard time understanding and accepting this statement. I had very low self-esteem. I did not know I had low self-esteem, because I masked it with a lot of bravado. But in reality, I was insecure and had a lot of fear.

I did not like myself very much either, so my subconscious thinking was, *how can I love someone else if I do not even like myself?*

When I turned thirty, I finally admitted defeat when it came to alcohol, and I checked myself into a 12-step program. One of the first things I heard there was, "Let us love you, until you learn to love yourself." This sounded like a foreign concept to me. But I realized right away these two things: That I desperately wanted to be loved, and that I really did hate myself. So what did I have to lose?

Maybe these 12-step people really could help me.

If you are at all familiar with the 12-step model, then you know that there are twelve suggested steps that lead us to a spiritual awakening and change from the inside out, which, in turn, leads to a life of recovery. Step eight says, *"Made a list of all persons we had harmed and became willing to make amends to them all."*

When I came to step eight in my recovery, I compiled my list as best I could. Then, in step nine, I started the long process of actually making the amends. Many of my amends were financial, consisting of making things right with people I had stolen from over the years—especially when I was a teenager. I started with my nine brothers and sisters. That was fairly easy.

One of my sisters, Shelle-Belle, even teased when I made my amends with her, "Does this mean that we can't call you Terrible Terence anymore?"

At one point, during the amends process, I was living and working in Helsinki, Finland, and I came across a self-help book, written by Melody Beattie. I still remember it was a beautiful Saturday afternoon. After I had gone to the gym and to the outdoor market for my weekly groceries, I was relaxing at home and reading this book. Beattie suggested that we have to make amends with ourselves *first*, before we make them with others. She said that we could not truly ask for forgiveness or forgive others until we first forgive *ourselves*.

I remember thinking that sounded impossible. How do I forgive myself? She did not explain any further in the book—just left me hanging. So, I thought about it for a while and I finally realized that I really had been my own worst enemy. I was a bully as a kid, and this carried over into my early adulthood. But at the root of it all, I was beating myself up far worse than anyone else. I constantly hated myself for all of the failures I experienced in my life. I was in my 30s by then, still single with no future prospects of marriage because I had proved over and over again that I did not know how to treat a woman. I had made so many mistakes. Life looked nothing like I had hoped it would.

And it was all my fault.

After contemplating Melanie's statement, I got up from my living room couch and walked into the bathroom where I gazed at myself in the mirror. With no hesitation, I said, *"Terry, I really am sorry for all of the shit that I've done to you over your life. Please forgive me."* I stared at my reflection a little bit longer, looking into my eyes. A little smile started to form on my mouth.

I walked out of the bathroom and cried for the next hour and a half.

I have never, and probably will never again, feel the relief of the weight of my own self-loathing that was lifted from my shoulders that day. I still had a lot of work to do, but I can honestly say that, since that day, I have never been the same. Praise God!

Years later, I was in a "funk." You know what I mean. Nothing was going my way. I hit every red light on the way home from work. I lost my car keys at a movie theater. Life was obviously against me.

My spiritual director at the time—a woman named Shirley—always told me that whatever my issue "du jour" was, I had to sit down and physically write about it. So on a glorious, Southern California day, my wife had gone to her mother's house with the kids, and I was home alone. As reluctant as I was, I knew I was in a funk, so I began writing. Once again, once I put pen to paper, and the pen started flying across the page.

I must have written 20 pages in about 45 minutes. I had no idea how much was on my mind until I started writing. I found that I was thinking about childhood issues, mostly having to do with my father. Why didn't he ever go to my baseball games like the other dads? Why did he have to drink so much? Why was he never at home?

As I wrote all of this down, I felt angrier than when I had started. So I called Shirley to ask what I should do with all the anger I was feeling. I got her voice answering machine. Frustrated, I called my sponsor, John. He was not in, either.

What was I supposed to do?

I called my dad, who was back in Boston. I asked him if I could talk frankly with him, man-to-man, so to speak. He asked me to wait a minute, as he had been taking a nap and wanted to sit up for this one. I prefaced the conversation by saying that I had been seeing a counselor and was writing as an exercise she had suggested. Then I asked him, "Dad, were you there for me when I was a kid? Because I really don't remember."

Without hesitation he replied, "No, I really wasn't. I was either playing cards with the boys or flying, and I really didn't take the time to be there for you kids." He went on to say, "I really thought that your older sisters would take you under their wing, but they did not. They had their own things going on."

I could not believe what I was hearing.

My dad was admitting that he had failed me as a father. I really wanted him to say that he was sorry, but that did not happen. However, just the acknowledgment was enormous in and of itself. I said, "Dad, that's okay. I just needed to know, because, quite honestly, my childhood is just a blur to me and I only remember bits and pieces of it."

"Okay, old pal," he said. Then we continued to talk about normal life stuff. When I hung up the phone, I felt like I was on cloud nine. My father had admitted to me that he was not a good father. If he had apologized it would have been icing on the cake. But men from that era did not often say they were sorry. And I was simply grateful for his honesty and openness. I could not wait to tell my wife when she got home.

I also left an excited voice message on Shirley's answering machine.

Two days later, my dad called to tell me that he had found a savings bond that he had purchased for one of the children. He said that he would put it in the mail and that I should have it later that week. And then the miracle happened. He said, "Oh, and by the way, that thing that we talked about the other day? I'm sorry."

We had struggled in our relationship for many years. I can honestly say that there were times I hated my dad. All of that hate ended when I went into my 12-step program and learned how to forgive myself and others. It took work. But, one of the best gifts I received in my recovery was that my dad and I had a great relationship from that day until the day he died.

Forgiveness is key.

I wrote in Chapter Two about it not being any of my business what other people think about me. Fast forward 25 years and six children later, my wife decided to divorce me. On top of that she poisoned our children toward me with lies, innuendo, and other smears. As of today, only one of the six will talk to me. So, did it initially matter to me what my children thought of me? It sure did. I was angry and frustrated. I did EVERYTHING for these children. For the half of you who are divorced, you know what I am talking about. I mean this woman, did not even have the guts to tell me she was divorcing me. This tale is truly amazing to me, and I by no means am trying to bash anyone.

As the brilliant nationally-syndicated talk show host Dennis Prager says, "What is the truth first. Tell me what the truth is first, and then we can dissect the issue at hand."

I had been separated from my wife for approximately nine months. I had been talking to a Christian friend of mine named Lyle about being prayed over. Again, if you have no religious background, then this will probably not make any sense to you. Lyle recommended that I go see a lady across town by the name of Connie. Connie and I set up a time to meet and, long story short, we went to the chapel at her church. She locked the door behind her, meaning no one else could come in. That shocked me, as I had never before been in a Chapel that was locked from the inside. She told me that she had the pastor's permission for her ministry. There was another lady in the room, as well. For the next 45 minutes, or so, they asked me questions about my life. Then they said they were ready to pray over me. Little did I know that this is what the Catholic Church calls a *deliverance*.

I was clueless.

For the next three hours these two wonderful ladies prayed over me. I don't remember all that transpired, however, I do know that Connie started out by saying; "Repeat after me." We did this exercise for a little bit, before she said, "Dad, I forgive you." I could not get the words out of my mouth. "Dad, I forgive you," Connie would repeat, in the same monotone voice. Even though my relationship with my old man had been sour for a long time, we both had made amends with each other, and life was good. Or so I thought. "Dad, I forgive you,"

Connie kept repeating. I could not—would not—repeat the words. This went on for at least 15 minutes. Connie never stopped. About every 15-20 seconds, the mantra from Connie kept coming. Finally, after about 20 minutes of this, I finally said the words, "Dad I forgive you," with tears and sweat running down my face.

And this was just the beginning. The next one was, "Mom, I forgive you." Oh, no, not her too, who used to punch us kids, and kick us, and for me especially use the belt across my back with vengeance. In fact, in one instance, both of my parents were whipping me at the same time. So, after my father's belt came down on my back, while he was winding up again, my mother's belt hit, and this continued to repeat itself.

Such was the life at 277 Adams Street.

For those readers who want to know what I could possibly have done to deserve such punishment. I had done nothing. Three of us had just walked down to the corner drug store for a vanilla coke and a package of three cholate chip cookies—25 cents total. We were walking home when one of the kids from a local boarding school, Milton Academy, unbeknownst to us, picked up a rock and threw it at a car, shattering a women's windshield, which in turn caused her to hit a street sign. Neither one of us knew why this other kid had done it, but like the military, at 277 Adams Street you were guilty first and proof of innocence did not matter. What was the point? The damage had already been done.

Needless to say, forgiving my mother in that setting took almost the same amount of time as it did with my father, "The General."

After three more hours of this *experience* in the Chapel, I drove back home. I was physically, mentally, and emotionally exhausted—completely drained. In fact, I was soaking wet from sweat. I sat down in my chair and began to go over it all in my mind, *What the hell just happened?*

The phone rang.

I thought, *Oh not now. Who is it?* It was my wife. She asked if we could meet down at the church as there was something she needed to talk about. I was barely able to get out of the chair, but I did. I put on a clean shirt and headed to the church. Long story short, she asked me for a legal separation, and I said fine. Then I said, "Wait until I tell you what just happened to me." But she had no interest and just turned around and left.

A week later a nice lady from the court came to my door with the court paperwork for the legal separation for me to sign. No big deal. But then, that same woman came back again the next week, knocking at my door. When I saw her, I laughed. "Don't you remember, you were just here a week ago. I signed that paperwork." She looked at me and said, "I think this one is different. Read the top." They were divorce papers.

My now ex-wife did not even have the guts to say the words to my face: "I want a divorce."

I do not intend this to be a gripe session, but I went into shock. This is the truth, so I can tell you how I was able to forgive her. Oh, by the way, this stay-at-home mom for 25 years continued shooting poison darts toward the children about me at will during our separation. But she got her divorce and her annulment and is engaged to be married.

Go figure.

So in shock, angry, pissed off, you name it, I had to get out of town. I moved to Naples, Florida. By the way, if you are ever in Naples, you must stop at the *Parrot* Restaurant, the best in town. So, there I was in my living room, day after day, praying and praying, asking Our Lord, "How can I ever forgive someone like this?"

Then *it* happened.

Again, if you are not familiar with spiritual things, you might not understand. However, I knew I needed to forgive my ex-wife, I just did not know how. So, after about a year and half of my mantra to God, asking Him how do I forgive her for what she's done, then one day, out of the blue, He answered me. Very boldly, I might add. He said; *"Terry, let me see if I have this right. You want me to forgive you your sins, but you're not willing to forgive the sins of others? Is that right?"* I forgave her that very moment!

Thank you, Lord!

Do you have someone in your life that you need to forgive? Is there someone that you need to ask for forgiveness? What are you waiting for? Is pride or ego getting in the way? Take the step. Make the amends and see what happens. Clean up your side of the street, no matter what the other person does. You will be internally and eternally grateful that you did.

I have included two more pieces of beauty for the end of this chapter. The first one is from Bishop Robert Barron and his website www.wordonfire.org. The second is a song from the band Supertramp that I really like. Check it out on YouTube.

Bishop Barron reflecting on the Gospel of that day.

Matthew 18:21 - 19:1

Friends, in today's Gospel, Jesus teaches the necessity of constant forgiveness. Forgiveness is an act and not an attitude. It is the active repairing of a broken relationship, even in the face of opposition, violence, or indifference. When a relationship is severed, each party should, in justice, do his part to reestablish the bond.

Forgiveness is the bearing of the other person's burden, moving toward him, even when he refuses to move an inch toward you. There is something relentless, even aggressive, about forgiveness, since it amounts to a refusal ever to give up on a relationship. Simon Peter asks Jesus, "Lord, if my brother sins against me, how often must I forgive him? As many as seven times?" Jesus replies: "I say to you, not seven times but seventy-seven times." Christians should never cease in our efforts to establish love.

Jesus' own startling practice of forgiving the sins of others emerges as one of the distinctive and most controversial elements in his ministry. And both rhetoric and practice reach their fullest expression when the crucified Jesus asks the Father to forgive those who are torturing him to death. We speak the truth because Jesus is the Truth; we forgive because he forgave.

Lord Is It Mine
Supertramp

I know that there's a reason why I need to be alone
I need to find a silent place that I can call my own
Is it mine, oh Lord is it mine?
You know I get so weary from the battles in this life

And there's many times it seems that you're the only hope in sight
Is it mine?
Oh Lord is it mine?
When everything's dark
And nothing seems right
There's nothing to win
And there's no need to fight
I never cease to wonder at the cruelty of this land
But it seems a time of sadness is a time to understand
Is it mine?
Oh Lord is it mine?
When everything's dark
And nothing seems right
You don't have to win
And there's no need to fight
If only I could find a way
To feel your sweetness through the day
The love that shines around me could be mine
So give us an answer, won't you?
We know what we have to do
There must be a thousand voices
Trying to get through

Source: LyricFind
Songwriters: Richard Davies / Roger Hodgson
Lord Is It Mine lyrics © Universal Music Publishing Group

CHAPTER FIFTEEN
Surrender Without Giving Up

"So submit yourselves to God. Resist the devil, and he will flee from you." — James 4:7 (NAB)

Surrender was not a word I heard very much about when I was growing up. I was taught that you had to be tough. You NEVER back down from a fight. You NEVER show your emotions. When I entered the Marine Corps, at the age of 18, surrender was not part of the vocabulary there, either. Surrender was the last thing we wanted to do. Our instructors in the Marine Corps taught us to never surrender.

So, for the majority of my life, I was a fighter, a scrapper if you will. In fact, I would do anything, except surrender. This has all changed for me, of course. However, that is what it was like growing up. I had to learn how to survive and grow up really fast. I later had to learn how to do a 180 and learn that, in life, I have to daily surrender those things over which I have no control.

One day, while traveling along the long canyon drive from the 405 freeway in Southern California to Laguna Beach, I was having one of "those" days. It was another one of those "funk" days. However, this day seemed worse than others. I just wanted to end it all. I did not know it at the time, but I was suffering from PTSD, depression and anxiety. I thought to myself, *Hey, I have life insurance. If I purposely fail to navigate one of these turns, I can end it all. My wife and kids will be taken care of.*

Obviously, I did not act on my thoughts. (Maybe Og Mandino was praying for me). I was too much of a chicken to go through with it anyway. Thank God. So, I navigated through the turns on the curvy road. However, that did not stop the feelings of depression and despair that were overwhelming me. Later in life, the spirit of suicide was prayed out of me, during one of my deliverances. But at the time of this story, thoughts of suicide sometimes occupied my head.

Later that day, I saw my good friend and sponsor, John. Frustrated from the recurring depressive thoughts, I told him about the thought I had while driving down the canyon earlier that day. I asked him, "John, when does it all end?" I wanted him to tell me when the pain would end. He looked at me, and said, very serenely, "Well, Terry," he often spoke in a soft voice, "You know when you are in the hospital, and that little line goes up and down and says beep, beep, beep? Well when that thing says *beeeeeeep*, then is silent. That's when it all ends." This sarcastic answer was not what I was looking for. But, thankfully, he went on to say, "However, if you are a believer, that is when life really begins." Once again, he was right. He was always right. He had a way of always saying the right thing, at the right time and always keeping things very simple so that I could understand them. Honest to God, when he spoke to

me, it was almost like parables.

He helped me to learn, to grow, over the years, to surrender to God all of the things I am powerless over. I have since learned that I am not in control of other people, places, things, situations, or events that take place around me. I have no power over how most things turn out. When I try to control everything, my life is often unmanageable.

Other times, I would go to John, whenever I was feeling my feelings and they were not good. He would always say, "Terry, are you trying to drive the bus? You know you need to let God drive the bus, and you go sit in the back seat." Interpretation: whenever I tried to take control of anything, I was driving the bus, trying to do things my way. However, if I just let go, and let God drive, while I sat in the back of the bus and enjoyed the view, things went very smoothly.

Does that mean you are a doormat now? Absolutely not! You are just letting the Big Guy drive the problem or situation, whatever it is that day. And He'll always give you the answer, if you listen and let Him.

I am, and we are, powerless and very much need to surrender the control to our God. For me, I had to stop fighting, kicking, and screaming when I didn't get my way. I have to realize that my way is not necessarily the only way. That was a big pill to swallow for me.

Am I successful at doing this? Not always. Especially when watching the news, which is why I rarely watch it anymore. It just gets me worked up. So much, it seems, is out of my control. So, I listen to music instead. So much better.

Remember, I come from a military family, one where I had to fend for myself. Then I went on to be a Marine. The concept of surrender definitely did not come naturally to me. But as I get older, surrendering is now much easier. My sponsor, John, wisely told me, when we first met, that all I have to do is change my life 180-degrees from the way I had been living it, and everything would be fine. Very funny, I thought. However, he was really telling me the truth. I had to do an about face with my concept of surrender.

Letting go of the control is so much better.

What areas in your life do you need to let go of? Write them down, and add to the list as new ones come up. Then try to let them go, one at a time. "Drop the rock," says my friend Paul. Let God drive the bus. You will be amazed at the freedom that you experience through surrender.

CHAPTER SIXTEEN
Amends

Help me look again at the people around me. Help me see the hurt and pain I have caused in others. Be with me to help me make amends for the harm I have done.
– Eleventh Station of the Cross

I freely admit that when I was a kid growing up I was not that honest. In grade school, I used to take orders from kids in my class for school supplies. I would then walk, empty handed, into the local 5 & 10 cent store, steal a green school bag, then pick up the school supplies that other kids ordered from me. I would put them in that school bag, and walk out of the store with all the stolen items, including the green school bag. The next day, at school, I would sell the items to my classmates at half price.

I even had a "store" at home, where I kept in stock things like Elmer's glue, rulers, pens and pencils, etc., and I would sell those items to my brothers, sisters, and the neighborhood kids where I lived. My older brothers and sisters could not understand how I could afford to buy all these things and then sell them for half price. How was I making any money?

I am confident that my siblings knew exactly what was going on, however, no one said a word to me about it. After all, they were all benefiting from half-price school supplies. Therefore, in my head, I could rationalize doing all of this in my multi-dysfunctional home. Remember the Sweeney motto, should you forget it, is: "We (the Sweeney kids) put the **fun** in dysfunction."

Now, here I was, twenty-five years later, and I had to make amends to all of my family and friends, including my parents. Naturally, they all forgave me immediately. I do remember one of my siblings, Rosebud, saying to me: "Your amends to me is that you just stay sober." Of the ten of us, Rosemary was the one born just after me, and probably took the brunt of most of my shortcomings, especially with all of her friends, some of whom I tried to cozy up to.

Then, it was time for me to make my *financial* amends. At the age of 14, I got a job at a local *Mobil* gas station.

Before I even started my first day, my older brother, handsome Chas, who worked at the Shell station, across the street, told me, "When you steal, steal lightly and often."

"What are you talking about," I asked him. I was clueless as to what he was talking about.

He replied, "When you steal money from the cash register, only take out $5.00 per day. No one will miss $5.00 a day, but they will miss it if you take out $10.00 every day."

So, I learned early on, not only how to steal cash, but how to be a con artist as well. That job only lasted me about four months, because I got greedy and started taking out $10.00 every day, despite my brother's warning.

I thought I was so smart. This was back in the day when gas station attendants actually pumped the gas into people's cars, checked their oil, and even washed their windshields. This particular gas station did not accept credit cards. The owner, Charlie Mullen, knew just about everyone in town. So, customers were allowed to set up credit accounts. It was not uncommon for customers to come in and get their gas, and whatever else they needed, sign a bill of receipt and leave. They would then receive a bill from Charlie at the end of each month. Even my parents had an account there. It was the norm. So, instead of stealing $10 out of the cash register, I would sometimes sign my dad's signature on a receipt as if he bought gas and take $10 from the till. I didn't think about him seeing *his* 'signature' on the bills that I signed. I should have just stayed with the $5 thing handsome Chas taught me, but I was too greedy.

I also had another method of stealing from the gas station. In those days, gas tanks were behind the license plate, not on the side of the car as they are today. So, we would actually steal gas by bringing our own two-and-a-half gallon gas cans, filling them up behind the cars we were supposed to be filling, then finally sticking the nozzle into the car and filling up the tank. We, of course, charged the customer for the entire amount. I never really felt bad about this, as gas was only $.29 a gallon in those days.

As I said, I was eventually fired for my dishonest behavior. That really sucked, because Mr. Mullin paid us in cash each week, and it sure was nice making your own money at 14.

In high school and college, my stealing progressed. I worked for a hardware store in Boston. The owner of the store, Herb, took Wednesday afternoons off, so I got to see hard core stealing for the first time. The manager of the store and his buddies were the worst. Yet, one more great con teacher! At first, I would grab a few things here and there, such as drills or jig saws, and I would sell them to my friends for half price. Or I would barter with the local barber for a haircut in exchange for some item. But, soon enough, that got old. Not the stealing, but the delivery of the goods I had stolen for my friends.

I got bolder.

I would charge my friends ten dollars each for a brown paper bag, and then let them go through the store to take whatever they needed for themselves, on those Wednesday afternoons. It was a lot less work for me, and they were happy as clams.

One day, the manager of the store, a super guy named Mel, asked me to start making deliveries to his buddies in the company van. I was also the delivery guy. I had *another* great idea of saving my friends the time of coming into the store, thinking I would just deliver the items they wanted, as well. I even hired my younger brother to come work with me. I taught him the ropes, just as my older brother had done for me. However, it seemed like he knew half of the stuff I was teaching him already! But there was nothing like working with my brother. We just had so much fun.

We were quite the crew.

This all came to a head for me in the summer of 1986. I had to admit that I was lying and cheating to just about everyone I knew, including my fellow Marines, my friends, and ultimately myself.

As part of my 12-step program, I had to make amends to those I had harmed. I was living in Southern California at the time. I realized that I owed amends to the owner of the gas station, the 5 & 10 cents store, and the hardware store. So that October, during a trip back to Boston to visit my family and to see the fall foliage, I knew it was time to make things right.

First, I went to the gas station. The owner who I had worked for—a great guy, Mr. Mullen—had died, and now his son was running the gas station. His son and I used to work together on different shifts. I walked in and told him why I was there and that I wanted to pay him back for everything I had taken. He nicely told me to get lost. He would not accept any money from me. He was just glad I was doing well and accepted my sincere apology.

Next, I went to the 5 & 10 cents store, just around the corner from the gas station. I asked the nice lady at the counter if I could speak with the owner. "Oh," she said. "Mr. Brackett died a few years ago. I am his wife. How can I help you?" I told her my story from my younger days. She too said that she would not accept any money. She also said that she was sure Mr. Brackett would have been very proud of me, had he been there.

Wow! I was feeling pretty good about myself. Things were really working out for me. Two financial amends down and I did not have to pay a dime out of my pocket. I was not expecting that.

Finally, I went to the hardware store. This was the big one. In my estimation, I owed them about $40,000, which I definitely did not have. Herb, the owner, was at lunch. So, I had to wait until he returned to the store. As I saw him coming around the corner, I started rationalizing in my head that maybe I didn't owe him that much. Maybe it was only $10,000. But I knew that was dishonest. Dishonesty was what had gotten me in this situation in the first place. So, I gathered up my courage and watched him walk in the door. He was a tough but very fair boss. If you worked hard, which I always did, he paid you well.

Herb saw me and looked genuinely happy to see me! "Terry," he said, "How are you? Gosh it's great to see you!" I had not seen him in at least ten years, so it was so great to see him, as well. I knew he would not be happy for long, once I told him what I had done. But I had to push forward. I had to drop the bomb.

I told him why I was there, what I was doing and why I was doing it. I told him that I thought I stole about $40,000 from him while I was working at his store. I admitted I was wrong and told him that I wanted to make it right. I acknowledged that I did not have enough money to pay back everything I owed him right now. I was just about to suggest some type of payment plan, when he jumped in and said; "Not you! I knew those other guys were stealing from me. But not you," He replied. I genuinely felt like a piece of dirt at that very moment. I disappointedly said, "Yup, me too. But I can start making monthly payments…."

He again stopped me in my tracks. "You are not going to pay me a dime." I could not believe my ears. Herb continued, "Just don't tell my wife." His wife did the books upstairs in the store. I promised him I wouldn't. He wasn't quite as happy at this point. I could see the disappointment on his face, because he now knew that I was also one of the thieves. He was sincerely disappointed about that. But he forgave me nonetheless.

When I left that store, I felt great, like a huge weight had been lifted from my shoulders, partially because I did not have to pay Herb back. That in itself was amazing. However, more importantly, I felt great because I had come clean. I had made things right with all the people I had harmed. In other words, I had cleaned my side of the street.

My relief in not having to pay back these financial amends was huge. But that is not always the case. We aren't always granted clemency. I deserved to have to pay them back, and I would have. But the Lord blessed me on that day.

The day I was dreading had turned out better than I could have dreamed. I believe there were two reasons why everything turned out so great. First, I was WILLING to make these amends. For me, that was half of the battle. Swallowing my pride and being willing to admit my wrongs, then trying to make things right. Second, my willingness became action. I actually did it. I looked at the people I had harmed in the eye and told them that I was sorry for what I had done, and I truly meant it. It was very humbling. And extremely healing.

Today, I no longer have to live my life as a lie. I work very hard to tell the truth, no matter what the cost. It is sometimes difficult because a lot of people today do not want to hear the truth.

However, today I try to avoid situations that in the past have required me to lie, and then have to eventually make it right. I try to do things right the first time. I try to always do the next right thing.

Do I have shortcomings? Absolutely! We all do. The important thing is how we handle those shortcomings or disappointments when they come in. Do you give in? Do you act on your instincts? Or do you pause and try to do things the right way first?

Now, if I get frustrated because I cannot get a prescription filled at the pharmacy faster than I think I should, because their stupid computers cannot get my address right, I still may say things to the girl behind the counter that I shouldn't say. I am definitely not perfect. But when I do realize what I am doing, I immediately say that I am sorry for my behavior. And I try to do better next time.

Do you owe anyone amends? Do you need to admit you are wrong and need to make things right with someone? Do you have a resentment against someone that you need to forgive? Are you willing to make amends to the people, places and things you have wronged?

From my personal experience, it is such a relief to get that monkey off your back. Be willing to swallow your pride and do it. Then take the action. Your life will become so much better.

And you will be a better person for it.

CHAPTER SEVENTEEN
Insecurity

"We have all at some point in life fallen into greater or lesser degree in this, comparing ourselves in that effort we have to know whether we are better or worse than another." – Silvana Ramos

Can anyone please tell me why approximately 80% - 85% of all woman, and 50% - 55% of all men, are so insecure? Why do people in general insist on comparing themselves with others? Now would be a good time to review Chapter two: "It's None of Your Business, What Other People Think About You."

In my entire life, I have only met one woman, a truly beautiful woman I might add, whom I have nicknamed Toby, who is completely comfortable in her own skin, (well maybe Pamala Gay Bennett, from Atlanta too, but that's another story). I actually met Toby this year (2020) as she and one of her best friends, who were like sisters almost, shared a spare bedroom in my flat, during the early stages of the Chinese virus crisis. No one knew what was going on or what was going to happen, so they asked me if they could crash at my place for a while. Not a problem, I told them.

Another thing about Toby is that she is gay, however I know that has nothing to do with her comfort level with herself. She is just a remarkable young lady, and I love her for that. In fact, I would venture to say, she has no idea how attractive this trait is to the opposite sex.

She once told me that when she was in High School, everyone knew that she was gay, but the boys kept trying to *hit* on her. I tried to explain to her that when someone like her is completely comfortable in their own skin, it is incredibly attractive to the opposite sex. As I said earlier, she is the only woman I have personally ever met who has this characteristic, and I feel blessed to have had the opportunity to meet her. While living with me, Toby confided in me many things that I am confident no one else knows, nor will they. For reasons unknown (or maybe known), we had an incredible bond with each other. She shared with me some of her secrets (see chapter 1) about her life, making her even more attractive, and I told her things about my life, that had formerly been secrets for me.

I truly believe I could write another book on just this topic alone, however, while during my research for this book, I have interviewed hundreds of men and women. I was able to compile some examples of how women responded, (see list below) and I got a lot of answers.

Additionally, insecurity is not just a female issue. Many boys/guys growing up, especially in the last two generations, millennials and now generation "Z," go through many of the same insecurity issues that woman do. Why? I truly believe that insecurity is one, if not, the biggest issue behind male and female behavior today. I even went online to look up books on the topic, however, would prefer to hear from my friends/readers on this topic, so I can blog about this on my website, www.terrysweeney.com, in order to help others.

Here are some of the responses I got, while doing my research:

> **Joy**: Woman in general are always comparing themselves with other women anyway. As a result, it is hard to 'measure up,' to what you perceive you should look like.
>
> **Rona**: I was never really good in school with math, so I feel insecure when I am doing my job and I have to calculate numbers. Or when I try to help my children

with their math homework. I just don't understand it. That makes me feel very insecure.

Karen: Social media certainly does not help a woman's self-esteem.

Grace: I was married to a man, and we had four children. The entire time I was married, I never felt secure with this man. I just didn't trust him. Thank God we are now divorced.

Shelia: Woman are their own worst critics anyway. When you look at any woman's magazine, it is filled with pages and pages of beautiful models/women. I know I will never be able to look like that. It's too unrealistic.

Sonya: With the availability of sex toys, vibrators, and free pornography on the Internet, most of my friends and I would prefer to just use these *toys* for our sex, and then get a dog, or a cat, for companionship. It just is not worth the hassle to us. I hate to admit this, but when we go for fun, we use guys.

Michelle: Every guy I've dated over the past year or so, has turned out to be a real jerk. I have never felt secure with anyone of them. I think they are more insecure than I am.

Candice: I'm overweight and have been ever since I was a child. I've always felt insecure about that. Now with raising children and working full time, I never have the time it takes to exercise or eat right.

This is just a sampling of my research. In fact, just this week, I read an article in the news about a woman in San Diego, who went to a dog park to walk her dog. She saw a couple at the park, who did not have their virus masks on.

She then took it upon herself to spray mace into the couple's face. What do you suppose are these women's insecurities? I am fairly certain they reach far beyond getting this Chinese virus.

I even interviewed one of my sisters, Bonnie, who had also worked as an attorney in the District Attorney's office in Boston. When I asked her about insecurity, she brought up the topic of menopause. She told me that she could be in the middle of a trial, and feel like she was going to drop dead unconscious. She told me it was just horrible. I believe her! I do not know that feeling, however, I reminded her that menopause was just something that a majority of woman have to go through in their life, that can *cause* insecurity. Once the symptoms of menopause were gone, however, I asked her, "Why are you still insecure today?" She could not give me the answer. "I don't know," she replied.

Unfortunately, Bonnie died while I was writing this book. She was another one of those just incredible women, like Toby, that I really got to know intimately over the past 10 years or so. Unfortunately, she never got help for the insanity we grew up in, like the rest of my other siblings, and died because of 'cardiac arrest,' however I know it was because she could not put the plug in the jug. Very sad as she was only 56.

The thing about menopause I told her, is that for most women, when it is over, the insecurity still remains. Therefore, I would really like to learn more about this topic, both from men and women, sharing about your own insecurities, and/or if you were ever able to overcome those insecurities, I know my staff would compile those answers, and pass them back to you, though our blog on our web site, www.terrysweeney.com.

Naturally, you can remain anonymous, if you do not mind, sharing your insecurities with us. Who knows, maybe we could get something going online whereby people share their insecurities, and others tell us how they overcame their own insecurities. Wouldn't that be awesome!

This book, and our follow-through, are all about helping each other become better people, and overcoming the obstacles that can and do hold us back from being the people we know we can be. I titled Chapter 8 "Are you the Best?" It is my belief, that if we can all work together, using my website as a conduit, we can help each other with whatever ails us. Thank you for taking the time to share your pearls or struggles on our website.

That alone speaks volumes about your character.

CHAPTER EIGHTEEN
Fear

"I prayed to the Lord, and He answered me. He freed me from all my fears." – Psalm 34:4 (NAB)

There is an acronym I heard way back regarding fear that I absolutely treasure. Fear is **F**alse **E**motions **A**ppearing **R**eal. In life it is good to have a healthy sense of fear. We all should have a healthy fear of our Lord. We should wear a seatbelt to keep us from going through the windshield, in case of an accident. Women usually carry their purses with shoulder strap over their shoulders to keep it safe from being stolen. These are all realistic fears.

What I am talking about is unhealthy fear. The Greek word is *"phobos,"* from which, of course, we get our word *phobia*. Many people go through their entire lives living in fear.

I've known several of these people. One of my other sisters is one of them. They are just absolutely afraid of everyone and everything. Why? Is it insecurity? Is it low self-esteem? What is the root of all of this fear?

I remember the first time I experienced the feeling of fear. I was six years old. My mother, who worked as a nurse at the time, was working her usual shift, from 3:00 p.m. to 11:00 p.m. at the local hospital. My older sisters would have to make dinner for my younger siblings and me, bathe us, and get us ready for bed.

On this particular evening, my father came home early. He was rip-roaring drunk, which was not unusual for him. What was unusual is that were all still up and awake. My older sisters had left to go do something after dinner and bathing us, and were not home when the old man came roaring in. In fact, my eight- year-old sister Shelle Belle was in charge of the five children under her, including me. We all ran upstairs to hide for fear of getting beaten by my father. He was screaming for Shelle, to come downstairs and make him dinner. As she got up and started to walk downstairs, I remember pulling on her leg, begging her not to go downstairs, because I was so afraid. I thought she was going to die. Then what would happen to the rest of us? If she dies who is going to protect us?

That was pretty intense fear!

She obviously didn't die that night. She did die before her time, though. I, however, will never forget the emotions and fear that I felt that night. I was emotionally scarred by this type of fear, because it happened so often. No child should ever have to experience that kind of fear, and yet it happens every day.

The next time I remember being really afraid was when I had to eject out of an RF-4 Phantom airplane, while flying back to Japan from the Philippines. In that moment I was extremely fearful because I believed that I only had about a minute or less to live. The first thought that went through my head, as I was being shot into the sky like a space shuttle was, "What a shitty way to die!"

I had done very poorly during this part of flight training in Pensacola, Florida. We all had been dumped into a pool while blindfolded, with all of our gear on, including our boots, so just keeping your head above water, with all that gear on, was hard enough. Then we had a parachute dropped over our heads. It took me several tries to get it right before my instructors finally passed me and allowed me to move on to the next pool training exercise. This one also included being blind folded again, in a simulated helicopter, then being dumped into the pool, and flipped upside down, while the helicopter was filling up with water. I did not do well at this part of the training, either, and had to repeat it several times, until I did get it right. The Navy, which trains all Marine Corps flyboys, was not going to let you climb into a multi-million-dollar jet, let alone land on one of their boats (aircraft carriers are referred to as 'the boat' in the Navy/Marine Corps) if you did not know what to do should you have to eject. Now, here I was in the air, as the plane headed towards the ocean.

This particular night, it was pitch black, with no moon when we ejected from the plane. I seriously believed that I was going to die of what we aviators at that time called FBI—*Frozen Ball Itis*. I knew I was about to land in 38-degree water, without my poopy suit on. A poopy suit, is similar to the wetsuit that surfers wear, but even better, as it goes all the way up your neck. We were required to wear our poopy suits when the water temperature and air temperature reached a certain measurement. They are truly life savers, however very difficult to wear underneath all your other gear, like your G-suit, vest, and jacket. In addition, I had no plans of ejecting that night. Now, in a flash, I was going to die.

I was about 25-years-old at the time, the same age as my dad was when he dropped the second atomic bomb on Nagasaki, ending WWII. Because we were flying into a Marine Corps base on mainland Japan, the second thought that went through my head as we ejected was, tomorrow's newspaper headlines will read "Nagasaki pilot's son dies in the Sea of Japan. Sweet Revenge."

But, by the grace of God, I ended up landing on the rock sea wall that surrounded the Marine base, with half of my parachute still not opened. As a result, several of the discs in my back were crushed, and I immediately went into shock. The experience was horrible. Just the thought of thinking you are going to die soon, as in less than a minute, is a horrible and frightening thing, in and of itself.

But I survived. I cheated death one more time, as we used to say after landing on the boat at night. I figured God was not done with me yet.

And I am so thankful that He still isn't!

The last example of a horrendous fear that I remember took place was when I elected to go to Russia with *the boys* one weekend when I was living in Helsinki, Finland. There was a train that left Helsinki for Leningrad (now called St. Petersburg) at approximately 3:30 pm each afternoon. I was already nervous to travel with my Finnish friends. A lot of Finns make this trek on the weekends, because it is a great, inexpensive trip where one can eat, drink and be merry. In comparison, it is the equivalent of a weekend trip from San Diego, CA. to Tijuana, Mexico. Rich place to a very poor place, where your money really stretches out.

I was nervous because I was traveling on a United States passport, while my friends had Finnish passports. For some reason I was terrified that I would be pulled aside when it came time for the train conductor to walk through and check tickets and passports. I had been in the reconnaissance/intelligence business for the previous 8 years. I had learned a lot about "Ivan's" ships, planes and tactics over the years.

Once underway, I relayed my fears to my friends, who just laughed at me. "Don't worry, we will take care of it," they said. But I was still worried that the Russians would find out who I was. Sure enough, when the conductor came by, and we handed him our passports and tickets, the conductor seemed to look very sternly at me. My buddies then broke out two packs of Marlboro cigarettes and handed them to the conductor. He immediately gave us our passports back and moved on to the next car.

"Oh, the art of persuasion," I thought. One has to remember that this was back in 1988, and communist Russia, at that time, was a big threat to U.S. supremacy. Sidebar: In my opinion, Russia will be an ally of ours if things really get out of hand.

But that wasn't the end of our adventure. That wasn't the half of it. My friends told me that when the train made its first stop in Russia, we were going to get off the train and exchange our Finnish Markka (no Euro yet) for Russian Rubles on the black market. This seemed way to risky to me. I do this in most of the other countries I travel to, including Israel, but not Russia! Sure enough, when the train stopped for about 10 minutes, my friends went behind the train station, where there was a group of about 5 men, who traded money on the black market.

I stood back and watched my friends make their deals, to ensure that everything was okay. Finally, feeling pretty secure about it, I walked up to one of the men to exchange my money. No sooner had I done this, when the KGB or whatever type of state police came out of the woods and descended on us in seconds. I was terrified. No one in the United States, and none of my friends or family, knew that I had gone to Russia for the weekend. I was afraid that I was going to be arrested, and when they found out that I was an American spy, I would never be heard from or seen again. It was one of the scariest moments in my life.

I had not yet been able to exchange my money, so when the men came out of the woods to arrest us, so I thought, I turned around as fast as I could, walking briskly back to the train. I was being followed by one of, what we call, the gray men that came out of the woods. I just knew that I was either going to die or spend the rest of my life in a prison in Siberia. I got on the train and one of the gray men followed me onto the train. I sat down and he just stood there, staring at me. "Is he going to arrest me or not?" I wondered. I technically had not done anything yet. However, you think they care about that in Russia?

At that moment, there was an announcement that the train would be leaving in one minute. My friends started returning to the train also. I had no idea what was happening. I had been so sure we were all going to be arrested. The KGB or gray men or whoever they were, including the guy watching me, simply walked off the train. Were we going to be okay?

As it turned out, these men wanted nothing to do with us. They were after the men who were dealing in black market currency. They had no idea how much fear they instilled in me that night, after all of my Russian studies.

Today, I no longer do these types of things. I try to live my life by doing the next right thing, every day. As a result, I no longer live in fear. I have learned to trust God in every aspect of my life.

Sometimes it is not easy. Are there times when I have felt that God has abandoned me? Naturally. But my dear friend Roy, may God bless his soul, taught me many things. The one thing he taught me that helped me the most, when I was at my lowest point, was to read the poem, *Footprints in the Sand*. When I feel like God isn't with me, I remember that during the hardest moments of my life He is the One who is actually carrying me.

I am so grateful that the Lord put true friends, like Roy, John, Joe, Fast Eddie, Nancy and Toby into my life. These men and women have helped me walk through fear. They've walked with me on this journey called life, when I needed them most. I have learned that most of the time, the things that I fear never happen anyway.

After all, fear is simply **F**alse **E**motions **A**ppearing **R**eal.

CHAPTER NINETEEN
Fidelity

"Blessed are the clean of heart, for they will see God."
– Matthew 5:8 (NAB)

One morning I was listening to one of my favorite talk shows, hosted by Dennis Prager. One of his guests was commenting on a book he had written. The guest said something that stuck with me. He told the listeners to ask your spouse, "What is one thing I have done for you that you most admire?"

So, one night, when my wife and I were driving to a party at our friend's house, I posed this question to her. I asked her to tell me what she admires most about me. She answered, "Three things come to mind right away. First, I admire your fidelity to me. I treasure that. Second, I admire your openness. And third, I love your willingness to grow." Needless to say, I was somewhat stunned and probably glowing with happiness at the same time.

It is important to note that before my wife and I were married, and long before we had even met, I was not the most faithful man in the world. Far from it. On at least one occasion, I know I was directly responsible for the death of an unborn child. My wife, on the other hand, was a virgin when I met her at age 28. She kept her virginity, as did my four daughters, until our wedding day. She gave me her virginity, which is, by far, the greatest gift a woman can give a man. We have also taught our four daughters how important chastity is before marriage. The two that have since married, were virgins when they married and the other two remain virgins. So, why do so many young women in our society get this part all wrong.

My wife's purity before marriage was an incredible gift to me. First, because she had the courage to stand for her beliefs, even when it was not the popular opinion. Which was especially true in Southern California. Second, it was important to me because I had, and still have, a nasty jealous streak. I feel fairly certain that I did not marry earlier in life, because my thought was that if a woman would have sex with me before marriage, who's to say she wouldn't have sex with a bunch of other guys, too? This may sound like crazy thinking, but it was true to me.

I wish I could say that I had replicated that gift of virginity for my wife on our wedding day. But my lifestyle up until that time had been anything but virginal. I felt like a hypocrite. What could I possibly give my wife that equaled the precious gift of virginity that she was giving me? Then it hit me. I can give her my fidelity. I could be completely faithful to her in my marriage. And I was. Thank you, Lord!

I know this is not a value that a lot of people hold onto in today's society. In fact, I have heard there are dating sites specifically for married couples to engage sexually with other married couples or individuals. Our society is in moral decay. It is no wonder that our country and our world is in the state it currently is. People have simply walked away from God and other traditional values.

So, I vowed to stay faithful.

Was this easy for me? For the most part it really was. We had six children as proof. Did temptation to stray ever strike me? Yes, it did—on two occasions. However, these episodes were superficial and never turned into anything that amounted to infidelity.

Working in the business world, I was required from time to time to meet with women for lunch or dinner. Most men and women in the business world are faced with these situations (pre-Chinese virus days). When this happened, I always invited my wife to come along. I would tell her ahead of time the day, time, and place of the meeting. Sometimes she came. Most times she did not as she was busy with the children. Sometimes these meetings were out of town and she was not able to attend. But I still invited her. I was always intentionally honest and forthcoming about who I would be meeting with. She always knew where I was, and could ask how it went. Putting this accountability in place helped me to keep my guard up against temptation, and made it much easier to have a business lunch or meeting.

I never, ever regretted my decision to stay faithful during my marriage. Life is so much simpler and happier when we keep our vows and live by certain moral standards and principles. When we keep our promises, people we love don't get hurt. Oh, and I never had to worry about jealousy, which, for a guy like me, was a big deal.

In addition, guys and gals, it is not too late for you to be a virgin, especially if you are living a promiscuous lifestyle now. It is still entirely possible to save yourself, from this day moving forward, for your future spouse. In Boston, we used to call this: "Giving away the milk for free." This means, that if you are a girl living with a guy, and you are not married, and you give this guy whatever he wants sexually, or otherwise, he will *never* make a commitment to marrying you (see Chapter 9 on Pornography). Why would he? He has everything he wants, and did not have to get married to get it! Heck, I have lots of friends in this situation who even have children together as well. That guy is never going to commit to a marriage. Almost guaranteed. Giving the milk away for free. That's what we called it. Made sense to me.

If you are married and are cheating on your spouse, are you willing to stop your behavior, and give that gift of fidelity to your spouse starting right now? It's a narrow gate when it's all said and done.

I remember one remarkable day. I was attending a men's group, known as *Christians in Commerce*. (CIC). I love attending men's groups, where we can gather together and learn about each other's struggles and feel confident in sharing our demented thoughts, as well as all of our joys, all without being judged. We can also share our own experiences with issues and give suggestions to other men on how to avoid struggles and pitfalls we ourselves have faced. It is very powerful. CIC is an international group, more prevalent in some areas of the country than others. When I lived in Oregon, there was no local chapter. So, I started one. Today I am blessed to live in an area of the country that has several CIC men's and women's chapters.

I remember this one particular meeting in Oregon that became a memorable and remarkable moment for me. We were discussing the subject of fidelity. Two men in the group, who had to be in their 70s or 80s, each shared separately that they had remained faithful to their wives for their entire marriages. And they thanked the Lord right there in the room, for the strength and courage to do so. Talk about an inspirational and powerful witness for me, in my early forties at the time. It was a value that just cemented my vow to my wife. Just hearing these guys' testimony that night helped to motivate and encourage me to stay the course.

God is so great. He often works in my life in ways like this. He puts people or situations in my life that point me in the right direction. I can either accept His guidance or not. That evening I was very grateful that I had taken the time to get involved in this wonderful organization.

CHAPTER TWENTY
Guilt

"Blessed is the one whose fault is removed; whose sin is forgiven." – Psalm 32:1 (NAB)

I am a baby boomer. I can't speak for other generations, but baby boomers' parents seemed to be especially gifted in the craft of giving others, guilt trips. My mother, Dorothy, fondly known as Dirty Dot, was the master of such guilt trips. She definitely would have won an Oscar for her role, had there been such a category. One of her favorite lines was; "And this is the thanks I get." Her other favorite was: "After all the things I've done for you…." This would be followed by a litany of all the wonderful things she claimed to have done for her children, of course followed by, "And this is the thanks that I get." Dot was very successful with all of us, but for me, it ended when I was about 16 years old. She lowered the boom on me one day, as usual, using her infamous lines. But instead of taking it in silence, I fired back, "Mom, I don't do guilt anymore. I'll do lunch with you anytime. But I won't let you make me feel guilty anymore." I think I got a black eye from that one, before she burst out laughing. But she never used those lines on me again. On top of that, after she punched me in the face, I told her that it doesn't hurt anymore.

She never hit me in the face again. Her belt was still very active though.

My dad wasn't any better. I was a military brat, and as such I was subjected to the Uniform Code of Military Justice (UCMJ). In other words, my father believed that people, including his children, were considered to be guilty until proven innocent. This is completely opposite from how the rest of the United States judicial system views guilt. In real life, people erred on the side of believing someone to be innocent until proven guilty.

Not in my house.

Unfortunately for me, up until about age 21 or so, I actually was guilty of about 90% of the "crimes" that I was accused of. With all of the baggage of guilt in my life, when it came time to raising my own children, it was hard not to say these same things to my own children. In fact, if I did try to go down the guilt trip road with them, my wife would say, "Okay Dorothy," to me, and that would put a cover on that bird cage. In my opinion, guilt crushes the spirit. I will never understand why some people insist on crushing the spirit of others, through guilt or any other message, especially those they are supposed to love the most. If we are guilty of crushing other peoples' spirits, we need to stop that right away!

I realize that I am not an expert. I'm sure that there are psychiatrists that can give me an intellectual explanation for guilt, its causes and reasons. And I'm sure this is important for some people, but for me, I am only interested in what *I* can do to stop guilt from crushing the spirit of others, especially children.

People feel guilt for all sorts of reasons. I knew of a Catholic guy that still feels guilty for eating a hot dog on the Friday they call Good, while at a baseball game in 1997. I also know men who feel guilty for the people they killed in war, mind you, lest they be killed themselves, while defending our beautiful country.

When people are struggling with guilt, I try my best to help them understand that they have to let go and let God. I tell them the same thing that was told to me, years ago. **Drop the rock**. Stop hanging onto all that crap you have been carrying around for so long, and it is all crap. Don't let guilt hold you back from living your life. We can't change the past, but the past does not have to dictate our present and our future.

Drop the rock my friends and move on with your life.

CHAPTER TWENTY-ONE
Resentments

"If you forgive others their transgressions, your heavenly Father will forgive you." – Matthew 6:14 (NAB)

I have a dear friend, named Jake, who grew up in Brooklyn, New York. I met Jake when I was in flight school, in Pensacola. FL. While growing up, he lived on the third floor of a tenement house with his five older brothers and sisters. One day, on his way home from school, one of the neighborhood kids came running up to him and said, "Hey Jake, are you guys getting new furniture in your flat?"

"Not to my knowledge," Jake said. "Why?"

The kid replied, "Because right now your old man is throwing all of your old furniture out the window."

As Jake relayed this story to me in Pensacola, he looked at me and said, "I guess the old man had a resentment towards the old lady that day." We had a good laugh, as I could easily identify with that kind of family drama.

I had many resentments during my childhood. There were so many incidents at 277 Adams Street that caused me anxiety and fear. It was not a fun way to grow up. One such incident occurred when I was about eight years old.

My mother was a nurse and she worked hard, typically working the 3:00 PM to 11:00 PM shift, either at the Carney Hospital or doing private duty. Her dream for many years was to have our kitchen repainted. We had old metal kitchen cabinets that she did not like. She saved her money for a few years, until she finally saved enough to have her "new" kitchen. She hired a company, and they came and did the work. When it was time to paint, she picked out a pleasant and cheery yellow color for the cabinets.

She was so happy when the workers completed the job. I still remember her joy that day. Later, she left for her usual afternoon nursing shift. A few hours later, my father came home. He was drunk, as usual, and was carrying six gallons of fluorescent, oil-based enamel paint. (For those of you who are not familiar with this type of paint, suffice it to say it does not wash off easily, as most other paints do today. You needed turpentine and a lot of elbow grease to remove this paint.)

My father had a gallon each of bright green, blue, red, orange, yellow, and purple enamel paint. Every color of the rainbow. He even had a few new paint brushes. He came into the den, where my siblings and I had been watching the Three Stooges and said, "Hey kids, mom is not really happy with how the kitchen came out. You guys should go in and paint away. It will make her happy."

Now, we were young. We had no reason to doubt my father's motives. We wanted mom to be happy. So, we each took a paint brush, and began splashing paint all over the place. Needless to say, it was a complete disaster. There was paint everywhere. We were covered with it, the floor was covered with it, the appliances and, of course, the kitchen cabinets.

Soon it was bedtime. So, after brushing our teeth and getting paint all over the sink, we crawled under our covers, smearing paint on our sheets. Of course, at that age, I didn't think anything of it. To my siblings and me, it had been a great night! We got to paint the kitchen and we made our mom happy! It was fun.

When my mother finally came home that night, it must have sounded like World War III had started. And my dad was simply sitting in his chair, smiling, with a cocktail in his hand. This was just another normal day in my childhood household. I now know how dysfunctional my parents were. I mean, what kind of person does that to their spouse, or to anyone for that matter? What adjective would you use to describe my father after this little caper of his? And this was just one of his stunts. Another one I remembered involved stealing toilet paper holders. You know, that piece of plastic that holds the toilet paper in place. We had five bathrooms in our house. So, the old man decided to take one of those holders, and throw it in the trash each week. The next week, he would do it in another bathroom, etc. Well, when you're a kid and you have to go, you don't care where the toilet paper is. You just want to make sure there is some in there. Who cares if it is sitting on the sink? You just didn't pay attention to that. Or at least boys don't. Then, my mother said one night at dinner, "Does anyone know where all the toilet paper holders are?" We all shrugged our shoulders, as we had no idea where they were or that they were even missing. We found out later, that this was just another one of my fathers "pranks." And this behavior was *NORMAL* at my house. I'm confident, as my psychiatrist told me, that this type of dysfunctional behavior definitely contributed to my PTSD diagnosis.

Unfortunately, I too know a thing or two about resentments. I learned first from my parents, and then became full of resentment myself. I'm pretty confident it was one of my biggest shortcomings as well. Add some jealousy and anger into the mix, and it was not a pretty sight. I also think that some of my siblings never got over this type of behavior either. We have all had our own battles with resentments, sometimes even towards each other. Remember the Sweeney motto: We put the fun in dysfunction. As for me, I chose alcohol and marijuana to numb the pain and noise of those days, as well as to fill the emptiness inside of me.

Thankfully, I was able to get sober and don't have to deal with nonsense anymore. NT (no time), Handsome Chas would always say. I did have to learn how to deal with resentments and work through them. In order to do this, I first had to admit to myself that I had this problem. That, in and of itself, was not easy for me. "I had been done wrong. Don't you get that!" I would say to myself on the inside. However, aside from working a 12-step program, I sought professional help as well. I also surrounded myself with loving and caring men and woman, who understood me, or had gone through similar things themselves and were able to offer their advice in order to help me. The most important thing that I found out about resentments, and my other shortcomings, was being *willing* to admit you have these shortcomings to begin with. It is possible to have peace where you used to have resentments and anger and bitterness toward others. Even if the situation hasn't changed, your perspective on it can change.

This is true for me today. Five of my six children have elected to not have a relationship with me as I write this. Yet, I don't have any resentments against them, whatsoever. I do not hold this against them at all. In fact, I love them all dearly. They may have resentments against me, but that doesn't have to rob me of my peace. I've made my amends to each one of them. I have cleaned my side of the street, so to speak. Time will tell if they are willing to do the same.

When it comes to resentment, whether it is a minor nuisance, or a mind consuming problem, it is important to let it go. If you hang on to them, they will eat you alive. Holding on to a resentment is like taking poison and then expecting the other person to die. Moreover, the person you resent probably does not even know it. So, they aren't bothered by your resentment towards them at all. You are the one who is losing sleep at night, who is distracted at work, who is consumed by the idea that you have been wronged. Resentments will kill you or at least give you ulcers.

Over the years I have become aware that some people easily get resentments against me, which is unfortunate. However, I come from Boston, where, like in other cities on the east coast, people tell it like it is. On the streets of Boston is where I learned how to survive. I didn't sugarcoat anything, especially the truth. I'm a straight shooter.

Often people do not know how to take me. When I first met my wife, and she invited me to family functions, they were definitely unsure about me. They were from Southern California, which is a completely different culture than the one I grew up in. They used to ask my then fiancé, "Why is he so angry?" She would have to explain to them that I was actually quite happy. This is just the way I am. I have quirky personality traits that can be a challenge for other people. They aren't flaws, just traits of mine that someone else might struggle with. It does not mean that I am a bad person, but my communication skills, for lack of a better term, are just different than people in the rest of the country.

My fiancé, turned wife, however was constantly defending and explaining my behavior and language to her family and friends. They acted as though I was from a foreign country, which coming from the east coast, in many ways is like being from a foreign country.

Growing up in Boston, the birthplace of the American revolution, we invariably viewed the world as if we were the best and the biggest. Just by where Massachusetts is located in the country, we inevitably looked down on the rest of the country. We are straight shooters, and most people on the west coast do not know how to handle this. They don't understand the way we are. They don't find our boldness attractive. But we don't change for anyone. If you want to get a good laugh, the next time you visit Boston, go to a souvenir shop and buy a map called: A Bostonians view of the world. I could not find it on the Internet, but it is truly hilarious.

I remember a story I heard years ago about Southern belles. Apparently, they are very good at putting people down and gossiping about others, so as long as they say, "Bless her heart" after whatever evil or gossip they have spewed, it is accepted.

I would rather be straight forward and say what I am thinking. I don't feel the need to hide behind nice words, afraid of offending people. If people don't like what I have to say, it's because, in the words of Jack Nicholson from the 1992 movie, *A Few Good Men*, "You can't handle the truth."

The most important lesson I have learned about resentments is that you can give people resentments, and you can get resentments from other people. The *key* however, is that *you cannot hold onto them*, or they will ruin your lives.

Life is too short to hold on to old hurts that aren't important. When we let these things take up too much space in our heads, we are only hurting ourselves. We have to admit that other people's actions are out of our control and surrender those resentments to God.

Then we can find peace.

CHAPTER TWENTY-TWO
Fellowship

"Therefore, encourage one another and build one another up, as indeed you do." I Thessalonians 5:11 (NAB)

Do you ever consider yourself to be lucky? Have you ever had one of those days where everything just went right? Maybe you got all green lights coming home from work? Or you found a $20 bill on the street?

Whenever I think about good luck, I think of one particular event that changed my life forever.

One day, when our first child was about six months old, my wife came home from church with a flyer for a "Life in the Spirit" seminar. She asked me if I would be interested in attending this seminar, which would be held on Sunday nights about 20 miles from where we lived. The seminar lasted six weeks.

Now, the last thing that I wanted to do for a month and a half on Sunday nights was go to some church thing. After all, I traveled often with my job. On a regular basis I had to travel as far away as Toronto from LA. Sometimes weekly. My idea of a perfect Sunday night was to light a fire in the fireplace, spend time with my wife and baby, have a nice dinner, put my pajamas on, and then settle in to watch 60 minutes. Needless to say, going to some church seminar was not high on my list of things to do. So, I asked my wife to put the flyer in my inbox at my home office. I would take a look at it later.

A few weeks later I miraculously had a week when I did not have to travel for work. I was so happy to be able to stay home and catch up on my paperwork. As I was plowing through my inbox, I saw the church flyer that my wife had put in there, three weeks earlier. I was about to crumple it up and throw it away, but something stopped me. I read the flyer again. I couldn't explain why, but I decided that I would give this a try. I told my wife that I would go, but only on the condition that she would come, too. She had already done the 'Life in the Spirit' seminar many years earlier. This was not easy, as our first bundle of joy, Eileen, was still nursing. But she agreed to go with me.

A few weeks later my wife, our baby, and I were on our way to the first of six meetings. We drove to the church and, when we got there, I was amazed at how full it was. Even more compelling were the people who were attending. The room was full of couples around our age, with small children. We fit right in.

The meeting began with praise and worship music, which I absolutely love. It reminded me of a Calvary Church I had attended once in the past. The music was great. "So far, so good," I thought.

Even more surprising to me was the fact that the people seemed to be genuinely having a great time, laughing, telling their personal testimonies, and sharing stories about how God had been working in their lives. I was blown away, as I had never experienced anything like this in any church I had been to. It was inspiring and the joy was contagious. I was very happy that I had elected to go to this seminar.

My wife had to leave the meeting early on, as the baby had become sick, so she just hung out outside. She had already done this seminar years ago, so she didn't mind. But I wanted more. I could not believe that I had found a place to actually enjoy being in communion with God. Before this experience I had not been very pious. I thought that the church experience had to be serious, and I was missing the point. We are supposed to enjoy our relationship with God. News to me.

On the drive home, my wife asked me if I was interested in returning to the seminar the following week. This was an easy question for me to answer. Of course, I was going back. I loved every bit of the experience.

The six-week seminar flew by, for me. I learned and experienced many new things, including being slain in the spirit, during the sixth, and last, meeting. I had seen this done on the televangelist shows on Sunday mornings, where people come to the altar, and the Pastor lays his hands on the person's head, and the person falls to the ground. I had always thought it was hocus pocus. But on that night, I experienced it, myself. I fell back, (they people behind you called catchers so you do not bang your head) slain, and I lay on the floor, unable to move. I had no desire to move, even if I could have. If fact, the meeting had now ended. People were putting chairs away and leaving, and I was still laying on the floor, with people walking over me, as in no big deal. They've seen this picture before. I hadn't. Eventually I was able to get up, light-headed, but erect.

At that last meeting, the leader of the group told us that on every Saturday morning he held a men's group. The group met at his house for an hour and a half. He simply called it a men's fellowship. I decided I would go and check it out.

I was delighted to discover that it was basically a mini version of what I experienced at the seminar. But it was a more intimate experience. We were a smaller group, and men were pouring out their hearts, freely speaking about the ugliest things they had done in their lives. No one was judged. Everyone was loved and accepted. It was a surreal experience for me, as I had never experienced anything like this before either, in any "church" setting.

As the meeting ended, we were invited to stay and be prayed over. This was another foreign concept for me. I had no idea what that was all about. After the meeting, I stayed for a little while, just to see what they were talking about. I watched for a little bit, then left.

Every Saturday I went back to this fellowship meeting. I was still slightly wary of the concept of being prayed over, so I never really stayed after the meeting was over. I also noted that during the meetings, many of these men had been praying and speaking in tongues. I had never even heard of that at this point in my life, much less seen it. I must have looked like a deer caught in the headlights on the freeway, the first time I saw this happen. Yet I kept coming back, week after week.

After I think my six or seventh fellowship meeting, I finally summoned up enough courage to stay after the meeting. I'd had a gnawing feeling in the pit of my stomach for quite some time. I could never really identify exactly what was causing this funk. I'd had it for years. That morning, I finally got up the courage to get up and sit in the chair that had been designated for those wishing to be prayed over. I do not remember a lot of details about what happened in the next few moments, but I remember that I started to cry. I had never cried in front of a group of men before, but for some reason, I did not mind. I also didn't know why I was crying. It just came out and actually felt good. In fact, it was beautiful.

On the drive home, while I was sitting at a red light, it hit me. The reason why I was crying. There had been something that happened in my life many years earlier. It was something that was left unresolved in my heart. It was something that I had never been able to come to grips with. That was what was causing my funk. That was what was causing that gnawing in my stomach for so long. I had never been able to identify the reason before those men prayed over me. I had stuffed my feelings so far down, and it was only through the power of God's love and the prayer of these men that these feelings began to come to the surface of my mind.

Years earlier, when I had gotten out of the Marine Corps, I took a job as a stockbroker in Laguna Beach, California. I had a small studio apartment that was right on the beach. I used to love going to sleep at night to the sound of the crashing waves against the sand. It was paradise. I was in my early thirties. I drove a fancy T-top sports car, and I was making good money. I did a lot of dating in those days. I was living the good life. At least I thought so at the time.

Although I dated a lot, it seemed like those dating relationships never worked out longer than a month or two. I didn't understand why. Was I the problem? Or was I just a poor judge of character.

One night, I met a girl from Boston. Her name was Shea. Being that we were both from Boston, I asked her if she would be interested in going out with me. We agreed and we went on a few dates. One night she invited me to stay at her place for the night. I did, and you know the rest of that story. We went out a few more time, but after a few weeks, things began to fizzle out. I, once again, felt that the relationship was not going anywhere, so I broke it off.

About three weeks later, Shea came to my office. She told me that we needed to talk. Thinking that she probably wanted to get back together, I agreed to walk outside to the backstreet behind the building where I worked. She looked me squarely in the eye and said, "I'm pregnant."

I was shocked. A million thoughts began racing through my mind, all at the same time. Is this real? Is she just saying this to get married? What am I supposed to do? I had no idea what was happening at that very moment. This was new and a first for me.

I told Shea that it was a lot to process and I needed a little time. I asked her if she would come back to the office the next day so we could talk more. She agreed and left. After she left, I returned to my office and proceeded to have a complete meltdown. You see, when I was a kid, back in Boston, if you got a girl pregnant you had to marry her. There just wasn't any question about it. Many of my friends had personally experienced this and now it was happening to me. But, how could I marry her? I barely knew her. I definitely didn't love her. I was panicking, thinking to myself, "What are you going to do now, Mr. Big Shot?"

It was then that my elderly statesman and co-worker, Howard, came into my office. Howard was the man who had so wisely advised me earlier in my life, "Don't die wondering," regarding whether or not I should go to Finland. He asked me what was going on. I guess it was pretty obvious that I was a basket case at that moment.

I told him what had just happened. He looked at me very serenely and said, "Terry, you do not have to marry her." Howard went on to say, "Terry, those days went out with the horse and buggy." (Apparently no one ever taught us that back in Boston.) Those words were a life saver for me. Once again, Howard's wisdom helped me one more time.

My next thought was to run. That is was I usually did when shit hit the fan. And my fan was on high speed right then. But for the first time in my life, that I remember, when the going got tough, I did not run.

Later that evening, I found out that Shea actually already had a boyfriend. He worked as a chef on a private yacht in San Diego. This made me very suspicious of her. Was she really pregnant? Was she just trying to make her boyfriend jealous? Did she have some sort of ulterior motive? Not much sleep that night.

The next day Shea came back to my office. We both went out to the backstreet again. I had made up my mind. I knew what I was going to do. I was not going to marry her, and I had to tell her that. So, I told Shea that no matter what she decided to do, that I would be there for her. I would support her in any way she wanted. Emotionally. Financially. Even as a co-parent, if that is what she wanted. But I was not going to marry her.

Shea just shrugged her shoulders, gave me a hug, and said goodbye. I never saw or heard from her again. I did not know if she really was pregnant and had an abortion or if she actually had the child. Over the years I have looked for her, from time to time. At one point I even looked for her in Hawaii, as I had heard she had moved to Maui. But to no avail.

All of this history came flooding back to me that Saturday morning after those men at the fellowship meeting prayed over me. In that moment, I knew that I needed to find out if Shea was truly pregnant by me and, if so, did she have an abortion. I realized that not knowing was why I had been walking around with that gnawing feeling in the pit of my stomach. It was not a coincidence that I suddenly remembered all of this after having just been prayed over. In addition, I knew exactly who to call, to find out if Shea had really been pregnant with a child. The traffic light turned green.

When I got home, I made the call. After some small talk about getting together with this old friend, I asked him if he knew what had happened to Shea. He answered me, "Yes, she had an abortion." I asked him how he could be so sure. He replied, "Because I paid for it." So now I knew.

After all these years I finally knew that my selfish and self-centered, carefree lifestyle was responsible for the death of a baby, and it probably contributed to the destruction of another woman's life, as well. That was a hard pill to swallow and it's been a heavy burden to carry ever since.

I struggled with whether or not to share this story with my readers. However, I can only hope and pray that God will take my mistakes, my foolishness, and my mess, and turn it into a message that helps others. He can turn my pain into something good, much like those men shared in our men's fellowship group.

The memory and guilt of this is something that I still deal with, and probably will for the rest of my life. But even though I view myself as a murderer, I do know that God forgives me. I don't deserve His grace. But He gives it to us anyway. I learned that because of fellowship with men who taught me about the love and forgiveness of God.

Before we had had our first child, my wife had suffered a couple of miscarriages, very much like my own mother. We named each child and had a funeral Mass said for each child as well. They are Seamus, Christian, and Shannon. Once I learned the truth about Shea, my wife told me I had to name the baby Shea aborted and we had to have another Mass said. I wholeheartedly agreed. I named her Kelly. How did I know she was a girl? It was revealed to me by the Holy Spirit. Naturally, as our children were growing up, they wanted to know all about their brothers and sisters in heaven. When it came to who Kelly was, my wife told them that I would have to tell them when they got to be a little older. So, when my wife and I decided each child was mature enough, probably around age 12 or 13, I'm guessing, I had the unpleasant distinction of taking each child out to lunch and tell them the story of who Kelly, their sister, was. Talk about another tough pill to swallow, looking at your child's face over a sandwich and letting them know the worst of the worst about you. It was very humbling, every single time, as we had six children. Each child was fully accepting and forgiving of my mistake. What a blessing.

Since that time, to this day, I have always been involved in some type of men's fellowship no matter where I've lived. I cannot live without it. That's how important it is to me. Ladies, I know there are several types of woman's fellowship programs as well. Just ask your priest, pastor or rabbi.

CHAPTER TWENTY-THREE
Listening

"…everyone should be quick to hear, slow to speak, slow to wrath…" — James 1:19 (NAB)

We live in the age of technology. No one can deny that we are communicating faster than we ever thought possible. Yet, while we are able to communicate with more efficiency and speed than ever before, the fact is that we aren't listening any better. In fact, our listening skills seem to be getting worse. The art of active listening seems to be a thing of the past. We tend to tune others out much faster than we used to.

Why do we have such a problem with listening to each other, today? Is it because the person who is talking is uninteresting? Or is it that we were never really taught how to listen in the first place. I definitely don't remember learning the art of listening in my school days.

Many of the leaders of the world, including presidents and CEO's of *Fortune 500* companies say that to be an effective leader you have to be a good listener. They would not have gotten to where they are today without listening to others and being open minded and willing to consider what others have to say.

My spiritual director, Shirley, was also a great listener as well as a very wise person. She is someone that I always tried to listen to. When I became a new dad, she gave me some incredible advice. She said, "Terry, I want you to listen with your eyes." Now, at the time I did not know what she meant. But a few years later I began to understand exactly what she was saying.

I remember one day I had taken the little ones to *McDonalds*. It was a Saturday morning and I wanted to give my wife a break, so I was allowing the kids to play on the *McDonalds* playground, to burn off some energy. While I was there, I noticed another dad there with his children. We apparently had the same idea. I settled in to watch my kids play, when I noticed that the other dad had brought along the morning newspaper. He was so engrossed in his reading that when his children came over to tell him how much fun they were having and tell him about their adventures, he barely acknowledged them. As they told him of their excitement about going down the slide, his nose stayed buried in the newspaper. It seemed that the articles he was reading were more important than listening to his children, and giving them the attention they desired.

My children would run up to me with the same excitement. They wanted to tell me and show me every fun thing that they were doing. They were so happy to get to have a burger, fries and a coke, and then play in the playland. And they wanted my attention through all of it. And I chose to listen, not just with my ears, but with my eyes. I would even get into the playland part with all the balls, not thinking about how germ infected that place was. I was a silly dad when it came to stuff like that. I would even take the girls on dates to get a manicure/pedicure, and allowed the workers to paint my toes, all to my girls delight. Another example of it's none of my business what other people think about me, walking around with bright red or green toenail polish on.

As my kids got older, they continued to want to talk to me about whatever was going on in their lives. They asked questions about any and everything. I tried to make it a priority in my life to stop what I was doing, whether it was reading the newspaper or doing yard work. I would get down on their eye level, and look into their eyes as they talked to me. I may not have known exactly what they meant or what they were talking about as they chattered on excitedly, but they always knew that they had my undivided attention.

Shirley truly did give me great advice when she told me to listen with my eyes.

Do you consider yourself to be a good listener? When others are talking are you truly focusing on what they are saying? Or are you more preoccupied with yourself, your opinion, or your response.

I once read a book by the famous pastor and motivational speaker Norman Vincent Peale, called *The Power of Positive Thinking*. It is a great book and I highly recommend it. In the book, Peale talks about a party he attended one evening. At this party he sat on the couch most of the evening. People would stop by, sit down, and simply talk to him. He stated that he barely said a word to any of these people who chatted with him. He simply listened to whatever it was they were talking about. A few days later he received a call from the host of the party. The host told him that everyone enjoyed talking to him. He went on to convey that Peale had, in fact, been the hit of the party. And he had simply listened.

Do you have the skill set that allows you to truly listen to others? While I do try to practice listening with my eyes, like I learned to do so many years ago, I still struggle with listening. If I'm honest I often interrupt people because something pops into my mind that relates to the conversation. I'm afraid that if I don't say it right then I might not remember it. And, of course, I want to give my two cents on whatever the subject is. Sometimes I interrupt because I believe the other person is ignorant or wrong about a subject and I want to inform him/her or prove to him/her that I am right. Ego?

It seems that when we truly listen to others, we show respect and care for them. When we give others our undivided attention, they feel as though they are important. This is a great gift we can give to others.

If you consider yourself to be a great listener, I would love to hear your ideas and tips on how others can improve in listening skills. Please go to my website, www.terrysweeney.com to share your experience and insights.

Thanks for listening.

CHAPTER TWENTY-FOUR
What Do You Stand For?

"When you know who you are and what you stand for, you stand in wisdom." – Oprah Winfrey

I once heard someone say that if you listen to enough people talk about enough subjects, it will be hard for you to determine what it is that you stand for. This sounds a lot to me of my college days, as well as Alexander Hamilton's quote, "Those who stand for nothing, fall for anything."

When I was in high school and college, we were taught that Marxism was the ideology of our enemies. My how things have changed, today. The educational systems in schools across America often teaching young people about the benefits of socialism, Marxism, and anti-capitalism. This is so sad to me, as we can look at any country that has tried this and every one of them, without exception, has been a complete failure. It is no wonder that so many young people today are lost, protesting and rioting against our current capitalist system.

I can't blame them for wanting to make their voices heard. I did the same thing in the late 1960s and early 1970s. In fact, my first arrest was on August 17, 1970. I was 14. I remember the date clearly because my friends and I went to see Janis Joplin perform at Harvard stadium for $2.00 each, in what turned out to be her last concert ever. She died less than two months later of a heroin overdose. I was arrested that night for, you guessed it, inciting to riot. However, we didn't have the looting and violence that we have today and we definitely did not disrespect the police. My friends had brought me back to my apartment after the show, (yes, I had my own apartment at 14) and told me to stay indoors. Not me. The adventure seeker had to see what was going on outside and eventually got caught up in the melee. I had not even started high school yet! That was not a pleasant call to the old man from jail.

It seems to me that there has been a shift in the way people think today. I blame it on our educational system, or lack thereof. People think they are entitled to things that they have not earned or worked for. Many people are looking for a handout. I definitely did not grow up like this. I learned very early on that if I wanted something or anything, I had to work to get the money to buy it. No one, especially not my parents, ever gave us a dime. I had nine brothers and sisters, and my parents did not have money left over after feeding, clothing, educating, paying the oil bill and the electricity bill, and sheltering us. So, we all just learned to work hard from the get go.

My parents knew a young couple who owned a huge apartment complex across the street from Harvard University. So, I was 13-years-old when I got my first job, cleaning and painting apartments, in Cambridge, MA. I walked a mile from my house to catch the trolly that took me to the train station. I took the train from the first stop, Ashmont through Boston, to the last stop at that time in Harvard Square. Then walked another half mile to the apartment building. One and half hours each way, to get to work and back at 13. But that is what you did if you wanted to earn money.

Entitlement was not in our dictionary.

Things are so different now. For example, when two of my children wanted to go out to see a movie they would ask, "Dad, can we have twenty dollars to go to the movies and get some popcorn?" And it was just expected that you would give them the money. Or one day, when my youngest daughter came home from volleyball practice, she told my wife and I that she needed a new pair of high-end sneakers for her games. And naturally they had to be a certain kind of volleyball shoes. I didn't have the money, but I was expected to buy the much-needed special volleyball sneakers, which cost over $100. Meanwhile, I was wearing my $35 sneakers.

I was happy to be able to do these things for my children. I just wished that my parents would have been able to do these things for me. But times were different then, just as they are different now. When I became a parent, I decided to do things differently than my parents. Today, your children *expect* things to be done for them and given to them. And this isn't just true in children, but in young adults as well. Today, we have children living with their parents until they are 25 – 35 years old, refusing to grow up and take responsibility for themselves. What's up with that? Parents have turned into enablers.

I remember a great story one of my friends told me when I first became a parent. He told me his rule with his children was that they could live at his house until they turned 25. If they were still living in the house on their 25th birthday, they had to move out. Well, as it happened, one of his daughters was getting married 4 months after her 25th birthday. So she asked my friend, her dad, if she could stay in the house until she got married. My friend told her no. Wow, that's harsh, I thought. His daughter moved out. After her wedding, and telling her dad that "she had her day," she told her dad, that moving out of the house was the best thing to ever happen to her. She told him, "I had to learn how to cook, how to clean, how to shop for groceries, how to pay the electric and water bills, you name it. It was great learning lesson for me." I thought he was harsh, at first, however I implemented the same 'rule' in my house. I never got the chance to apply it however, as the misses divorced me.

Recently, I had a date with a very nice woman. She was a widower with three daughters. Over lunch, that afternoon, this woman told me that her 18-year-old daughter ruled the house. I asked her why she would allow that in her home. She did not have a clear answer. The best she could muster was; "She's a *Millennial*," while shrugging her shoulders. As if that explained and justified it. I could not believe what I was hearing. That would never have happened in my house.

Unfortunately, that is the attitude of many young people these days. An air of entitlement abounds in younger generations. Politicians such as Bernie Sanders, who is a self-described socialist, thinks that certain things should be given away for free. I do not see how this could possibly work for our good. Someone has to pay for these things, and not the U.S. Government.

The track record for success in socialist nations is pretty piss poor, as well. Look at places like Cuba or Venezuela. Their economies are suffering and the people are starving to death daily. Canada and the UK both have socialized medicine.

While people technically have access to free healthcare in those two countries, the queue to see a doctor in these countries is extensively long. On top of that, the healthcare is rationed and not everything is covered. Canadians with access to more money often come to the United States to get the treatment that they need, and cannot get in their country. The health care system in either country does not work. Just ask the people who live there.

When I lived in Naples Florida, I often used ride sharing companies, such as *Uber* or *Lyft*, to get around town. I will never forget one night when a Cuban driver, a woman named Lolita, picked me up. She was a 37-year-old mother of two children. I asked her how she got into the United States. It was not a pretty story, but very similar to my cleaning lady and every other Cuban person I spoke with in and around Naples. People from Cuba are willing to do *anything* to get out of the socialist dictatorship that is their country.

Lolita was thrilled to be in the United States. During the recent riots and protests, she mused, "Let them go down to Cuba for a month, and then see if they still want to protest what they have here." I had to agree with her. I've travelled to Cuba several times when I was in the Marine Corps. She is not lying.

I think that people who want socialism in our country should visit Cuba or Venezuela for a month and then see if they still like it. I think if they saw socialism in reality, then they would change their tune in a heartbeat.

Not only has our education system changed, but also journalism and news media has changed. It seems to me that the general media institutions of today, whether left or right, whether on television, radio or in print, have spun out of control. The media today presents news to get ratings, which gets them advertising dollars. They simply don't care if you sit in front of your television and they flat out lie to your face. That is not the way it was for my generation. Back then it was called journalism. Back then the news was factual, and not biased to serve its audience. However, with the current twenty-four hour news programming, as well as online access to up-to-the- minute news on the internet, the only thing media outlets today are concerned about is the almighty dollar, not hard facts. That, in turn, provokes public interest and excitement, at the expense of accuracy. It is sensationalized, on both the left and the right. Facts are skewed and stretched to fit a narrative. This is not true journalism. Today it is hard to know what is truth and what is opinion.

When I was a child, I would see my dad watch the news with Walter Cronkite or Dan Rather. Back then we knew that the news anchor was a straight shooter. Today, people believe what they see and hear on the news, in print, and even on social media, without searching for the actual facts. They blindly accept what they are fed.

So sad.

I personally do not watch the news anymore. I listen to music instead. So much nicer. In addition, I subscribe to the *Wall Street Journal*, because they offer information about business and markets, and their editorial pages and their news is straight forward. There is no political agenda. They simply report the truth. It's marvelous! Like the print media was when I was young.

I also follow a couple of websites, to stay informed. I visit foxnews.com, just to see if the world has blown up yet. I also like to look the drudgereport.com from time to time. Drudge is a compilation of all the idiotic things that occur in the U.S. and around the world daily. I also like the easy access to other people's sites, such as Maureen Dowd, Peggy Noonan, Paul Krugman, and George Will. Articles from the *Drudge Report* can often be considered doom and gloom, so I always read it all with a grain of salt, and I try not to spend too much time focusing on the negativity presented in our world. Just the funny news for me, thank you.

I don't take any news articles too seriously, in order to keep my sanity. Today, almost every media outlet has their own agenda, and I try not to get sucked in to any extreme opinion so I don't fall into the trap! Paul Simon sings, in his song, *The*

Only Living Boy in New York, "All the news I ever need is in the weather report." He's got it right. And that was recorded in 1970, 50 years ago!

Talk about being ahead of the times.

We always have the option of what we take a stand on. Sometimes it is hard to discern which side is right and which side is wrong. So, we must study and learn and pay attention to *facts* and the *truth.*

As an example, when I was younger, I did not have an opinion on the pro-choice/pro-life debate, as no one taught me about this. I knew nothing about the topic, and did not even give it any consideration until I was 34-years-old, when my fiancé taught me the truth about the issue.

By that time, I had already gotten a previous girlfriend pregnant, and she had elected to have an abortion. I was absolutely powerless in that situation. And while I did not like that I did not have a say in what my girlfriend at the time, elected to do, I was not pro-life either. I was nothing, as I knew nothing about the subject. I was absolutely oblivious to all of it. Until I became willing to become informed and to learn the truth.

In my opinion, men cannot even comprehend what it is like for a woman to carry a new life inside her body. As of this writing, both of my married daughters are pregnant. Only a woman can know the joy of having a living child with a heartbeat inside her. So, once I learned the truth about abortion, I now have taken a stand for what I believe in and I am pro-life.

Take a stand for what you believe in and do not back down. Learn everything there is to know about an issue, so you can defend your position when the opposing side comes after you. Because no matter what the topic or issue, there will always be an opposing side.

When Donald Trump was first running for president, I went to one of his rallies, in Costa Mesa, California. Naturally, there were protesters there, carrying signs. I saw one young kid holding a sign, and I could not quite understand what the sign was saying. I could not figure out exactly what the man was protesting. So, I asked him, "What exactly are you protesting?"

He simply answered, "Read the sign."

I told him I had read it a few times, and I was sincerely trying to figure out what his message was. I asked him, "Can you just tell me what you are trying to say?"

He, again, replied, "Read the sign."

I began to get frustrated, but then it dawned on me. He had no idea what was on the sign either. He was a paid protester. Protesters at these rallies make between $50 to $100 per day, just for carrying a sign. I guess it's an easy way to make money. But I don't think he cared at all about what he was protesting. He didn't even know, himself. So if you do watch the news, bear in mind that most of the protesters are just there to make a buck.

What are you passionate about? What do you stand for? I asked my wife this question early on in our marriage. That was an easy question for her to answer. She promptly rattled off at least ten issues that she felt very strongly about. And over the years, in her daily life, she proved to the entire family, that she did stand for those issues.

My older brother is also someone who comes to mind when it comes to taking a stand. He went to Harvard Divinity School. There was a time, many years ago, when he lived with me in Laguna Beach. He was a good man with a big heart. I remember that he always had a special admiration for the late Dr. Martin Luther King Jr. He was inspired by him and the work that he had done in the 1960s. It came to my brother's attention, that while many cities and states across the country recognized a Monday in January each year to honor and remember Dr. King, Laguna Beach did not recognize this holiday at the time.

My brother wanted to change this. He took a stand for what was important to him. He petitioned City Hall and organized a protest. He organized it all. He created flyers and had them printed and distributed around the town. He visited the various community colleges in the area and asked the students to help him make signs for the protest. He passionately poured his heart into his convictions and it was clear because of his actions. He did not keep his opinions and intentions to himself. He acted on them to change things for the better.

Initially, his endeavors were not successful. But he kept doing the work. He kept pushing for his goal. And eventually, Laguna Beach began to recognize the January holiday that honored the late Dr. Martin Luther King Jr.

He took a stand for an issue that he believed in. What about you? What things do you stand for? What causes and issues are you passionate about? Or, are you content to believe in nothing, so you will fall for anything? Are you more like the paid protestor who holds a sign for money, with no idea what he is fighting for? Or do you take a stand and take action? I don't believe that we should ever let others dictate how we should view the events and issues that are going on around us. When we see things that are wrong in society around us,

we need to arm ourselves with information **and truth** and then take action to make the world a better place.

CHAPTER TWENTY-FIVE
Trust

"In God We Trust; All Others Pay Cash"
– Jean Shepherd

In whom do you trust? Do you trust anyone? Do you trust some people, but not others? How does someone earn your trust?

When I was growing up just outside of Boston in the 1960s, I learned very early in life to not trust *anyone*. If you never trusted anyone, then you wouldn't get hurt. That is what I learned early on. In addition, your chances of getting ripped off would be greatly reduced. Conversely, it was only when people trusted me that I ripped them off.

I can think of a great illustration of this. My brother and I had our own rooms in the attic of our huge house. The house was so old, that the attic bathroom had a chain that had to be pulled down to flush the toilet. The water tank was actually stored *above* the toilet, up by the ceiling.

I had my own room with a telephone in it, which was a really big deal. That too was awesome. One day, when I was about 17-years-old, I went down to the local bank and applied for a $2,000 loan. The bank employee asked me to fill out some forms. When I got to the application question about work, I simply made up a company. I wrote "Northeast Contracting" and put the phone number in my room as the office phone number. Sure enough, about an hour later the phone rang. I disguised my voice, answering by saying, "Northeast." The bank employee asked me if I had an employee by the name of Terry Sweeney.

I answered, "Oh Terry. Hell of a guy," as I rattled some newspapers. She asked how much I made each week. I gave her a dollar amount, one dollar higher per hour than I had put down on the application, to give the impression that the boss thought I was worth more. I had to get the bank to buy into the idea that this was the real deal. That was part of the con. I learned a lot about life from my older brother Handsome Chas, from the 1973 movie, *The Sting*, which won the Best Picture Oscar that year, as well as *American Hustle*, years later. Two great movies I would recommend to anyone over 14 years of age.

"Thank you very much," said the bank employee, and then she hung up the phone. The next day I was approved for the

$2,000 loan. I went in and signed the papers. I cashed the check right then and there and by five o'clock that afternoon I was at Darcy's pub. I had a wad of cash and was buying rounds of beer for the boys. I later went down to the *Eire Pub* in Dorchester and did the same thing.

Everyone was asking me about how I made my money. "Legitimately," I said. Well, in my mind it was legitimate, because I had every intention of paying it back. While at *Darcy's*, the hooligans and vultures started circling like birds of prey. They wanted to know if I would answer the phone and pretend that they worked at "Northeast Contracting," as well, so they could get loans. I told them that I absolutely would—for a fee of ten percent. That was the first number that went through my head, and everyone just agreed to it.

I can't believe this scam worked. It helped me pay off my original loan, so I could go back and get a larger loan. It was none of my concern whether or not my friends paid back their loans, even my older brother, had no intention of paying his back. I did have to change my phone number though when the bank, then bill collectors, started calling.

My point in telling this story is that I didn't trust anyone. And I wasn't trustworthy either. I could con anyone into trusting me, though. In fact, on the day after my wedding, I had given my dad my tuxedo to drop off at my wife's parents' house. He had rented a convertible, and a couple of my sisters were with him. They had never been to California before. They stayed in the car, while my dad went inside to drop off his and my tuxedos. My new in-laws were raving to my father about how much they loved me and what a great guy I was.

He could not believe his ears.

When my father got back to the car, he told my sisters, "Boy, has Terry got them conned." Thanks, Dad!

Today my life is completely different. I have many people whom I trust and who trust me. I do think it is harder for men to trust other men and I am grateful that I have several men in my life whom I completely trust. It appears to me that, women find it easier to trust other women than men. Maybe, maybe not. I think it takes men longer, and there has to be strong fellowship to forge this kind of bond.

We've all heard the old adage that says, "Love conquers all." Well, I think it is a cliche and totally untrue. I believe that *trust* conquers all. Without trust, love can't exist. Regardless of how much someone loves another person, that love will eventually die if there is betrayal of trust.

Love can only conquer all when there is trust, in my humble opinion.

CHAPTER TWENTY-SIX
Goals and the Subconscious Mind

"Focus on the possibilities for success not on the potential for failure." — Napoleon Hill

In the apartment complex where I currently live there are many young adults between the ages of say 19-35 years old. If I'm down at the pool, I'll usually strike up a conversation with them. I typically ask them about their careers. For example, I asked this young guy what he did for a living and he told me that he fries chicken all day in a fast food restaurant. Then I asked, "But, what do you see yourself doing when you're 25- years-old?" He had told me he was 21.

"Oh, I want to be an Automotive Service Excellence (ASE) mechanic."

"Have you finished high school?"

"Well, no. Not yet," he said.

It's a fairly typical response. Pretty scary huh? The very next day, I handed this young man the email address and phone number of the guidance counselor at the high school he told me that he had attended. "Give her a call today or tomorrow," I told him. I had called the school he told me he had attended as soon as I got back from the pool to get the information. I said. "She will tell you what you need to do to finish." Sadly, in the two months since I gave him that information, he has not contacted the guidance counselor.

I guess he'll be frying chicken for quite some time.

One young lady, 20 years old, told me that she wanted to finish her high school degree before age 21, so she could be a *bud*tender—someone who sells marijuana from a store. She told me that she only had three credits left to go to finish to get her high school diploma. I did some research and found a free program online for her to complete the necessary coursework. I even told her I would help navigate the website. I was actually curious to know for myself what they are teaching in public high schools these days.

I never heard back from her since that day.

In yet another example, I met a gal who told me she was 25-years-old and had a small child, though she had never married. She was having a chronic argument with her boyfriend, so he was not allowed to spend any nights at her house. She would let him come and take their daughter on dates, or to the park, so that's a good thing. She told me all about her bucket list items, things she wants to accomplish in her life. One of those items was a trip to New Zealand.

Frankly, I have my doubts that she will ever actually make it out of the United States. Maybe, just maybe, if these kids, or anyone else used some simple guidelines about setting and meeting your life goals, or any goal for that matter, life would change for the better.

I learned all about this from this incredible lady named Toni Taylor. Toni was a life coach when I met her. She taught classes about how to set attainable goals for yourself. There was a new coaching class coming up in a month. Even better, the classes were being held at a place close to the Marine Corps base where I was stationed at the time. I decided to give it a go, since the classes were in the early evening, which worked out great for me. I usually finished work around 1800 hours (6:00 p.m.), which gave me 45 minutes to drive through *In and Out Burgers* for a quick dinner.

For those of you who live east of Arizona, and have never heard of *In and Out*, you've missed the best burgers in the world. Now, there's a bucket list item for you! We're very spoiled out here.

But I digress.

I decided to give her class a shot. It turned out to be one of the best decisions I have ever made. In the interest of full disclosure, Toni had three beautiful daughters, somewhat around my age, who sometimes assisted her with the classes. I would have been happy to date any of them. But I never got that chance. I did get the chance to attend Mass and see St. John Paul II with one of her daughters Jane though, at the Los Angeles Coliseum in 1987. That was an amazing event, too.

Back to goal setting. Toni gave us a blue sheet of paper one day. I still have mine 35 years later. She told the class, "I would like you to write down ten of your most outrageous goals, even if you know the possibility of these goals becoming true is unrealistic. Being originally from Boston, I wrote down things like play one year for the Boston Celtics basketball team, play one year in the outfield for the Boston Red Sox, and play on the first line of the Boston Bruins hockey team, among other things.

I was just having fun as she suggested.

When we finished this exercise, she then handed us another piece of blue paper (I guess she liked blue), however this time, we were to write down ten *realistic* goals. That was not too hard, either, because I wanted to get married and start a family, buy a house, and buy a convertible *Volvo*, among other things. After writing all of my realistic goals down, Toni gave us the kicker. She told us to go out and get one of those big white poster boards and get a picture or pictures of what we had written down on the realistic list. So, I went to *Wal-Mart* to get my poster-board. Then I looked for pictures in magazines and such. I am happy to report that everything on my list, and I mean everything came true. Now, I did not get the convertible Volvo until 20 years later, but I got it, nevertheless. I had no idea how powerful *written* goals could be—and, yes, they must be written down. The white board was for the *subconscious mind*.

I also learned how powerful the subconscious mind can be from another guy who was a dog handler during the Vietnam war. Dogs can smell and hear things about 1,000 times better than humans. As a result, he was able to guide teams though the jungle, while the dogs sniffed out snipers or the enemy from a safe distance. These dog handlers had heavy bounties on them during the war.

I forget the dog handler's name, but I remember that he taught classes on the subconscious mind. A lady from my church coaxed me to go to one of his seminars. It was on a Sunday. I went reluctantly, after having paid $110 dollars, but I had a "we'll see" attitude. Most of the people in the room were there for their third, fourth, and even tenth time. Why? I thought to myself. In the class, if you were new, you had to sit in the front row. No big deal. I actually got to sit next to a professional football player. Now there were some stories.

About ten minutes into his lecture, I was writing down notes like crazy. I didn't want to lose any of the pearls this instructor was sharing. When he saw what I was doing, he looked at me and said, 'What are writing down?"

I told him that I was a slow learner, so I needed to write down as much as I could. He then stared at me and said, "If I said that to one of your children, what would you do to me?"

I replied, "I'd put a beat on you, pretty badly."

He was teaching me how powerful the subconscious mind can be.

When I was a kid, someone, I really can't recall who—maybe a teacher or my mother—labeled me as a slow learner. I heard it when I was around eight or nine years old. That one line stuck with me in my subconscious mind, since that young age. But it wasn't true. However, in my subconscious mind, I believed I was a slow learner, until that day in class. I learned that day that I was *not* a slow learner. That is how powerful the subconscious mind really is. So, from age nine, to age fifty-five, my subconscious mind was telling me that I was a slow learner.

I now knew instantly how powerful the subconscious mind really is. And this was just in the first ten minutes of the class! In actuality, all I had to do was look back on all my accomplishments over the years, to know that life-long label wasn't true. I think it was Norman Vincent Peale who said that as soon as we say something negative about ourselves, we should immediately counter it with a positive thought. I wholeheartedly agree, as this was just one example of how powerful the subconscious mind works. Don't ever say negative things, especially about yourself, to yourself. If you do, immediately counter it with something positive. This guy taught us that every image that goes into our mind, should be Pure, Positive, Productive, and Powerful. You want positive things about yourself in your subconscious mind, not all that negative crap. So, here's an example. Sometimes I will look at myself in the mirror after taking a shower, and say to myself, "Man, you are getting fat." Now, most guys do not really care about stuff like that. I know my friend Toby didn't, as she was so comfortable with herself. However, as soon as I say that to myself, I counter it with something positive, such as, "Man, you are looking really good today. Maybe you could drop a few pounds here or there, but overall you are looking good." You *must* immediately counter whatever negativity you are feeding or have fed to your subconscious mind, with something positive, right away. This way your subconscious mind is filled with beautiful and truthful thoughts instead of things like, 'you're a slow learner,' for 46 years, folks. That is what I believed from one statement I heard about me at age 9! Get rid of that stuff now!

CHAPTER TWENTY-SEVEN
Entitlement

"Nothing guarantees more the erosion of character than getting something for nothing." – Dennis Prager

You may have noticed that in Chapter 24 (*What do you stand for?*) and Chapter 10 (*Anger*) the underlying theme is *entitlement*. These days it seems that people often feel entitled to anything and everything. I'm not sure where this attitude of entitlement comes from. The Progressive party of Bernie Sanders and company, I suppose, but it seems to have permeated the minds and perspectives of an entire generation.

It is a fact that if you go into any military branch of service and serve at least four years, you are entitled to some type of college benefits. I do not know the specifics. I think they call it the revised GI Bill. However, I do know you get these benefits because you have worked for the military by serving your country. This makes perfect sense to me. It also seems very reasonable. If you serve your country, you have access to a better education.

Many young people these days are being swayed by the idea of socialism. They believe that everything should be handed to them on a silver platter, without doing anything in return. This kind of attitude was not prevalent when I was growing up. Yet, my father felt he was entitled to do any and everything that he wanted, however he had two jobs as well. So, I learned part of this behavior and thinking very early on.

My father was famous for parking in places that had "No Parking" signs in and around Boston. He regularly ran red lights, because he couldn't be bothered to obey traffic laws. He would cut in lines at stores. Nothing, absolutely nothing, seemed to matter to him.

He was "The General," after all.

If you opened the glove box in his car, it would not be uncommon to see it filled with as many as 25 parking tickets. One day I asked him what he was going to do with all the parking tickets he had. He simply said, "Give them to Dick." Dick was Richard McLaughlin, who was the Registrar of Motor Vehicles in Massachusetts at the time. He was also a Colonel serving under my dad in the Massachusetts Air

National Guard. He was also the Godfather to one of my sisters. So, my father's answer made perfect sense to me.

One time, when I was 14-years-old, my friend, whom we called Mr. C, and I, along with my dad and Dick, were driving down to Cape Cod for drill weekend at Otis Air Force base. My dad was the base commander. It was about a 70-minute drive to the Cape from Boston. About 20 minutes into the drive, my dad pulled off to the side of the road. He and Dick got out of the car and told us to trade places with them. They proceeded to get into the backseat of the car so they could drink. "Terry, you drive," Dad said.

Remember, I was only 14 years old and had no driver's license, though I had already learned how to drive. Mr. C., who was 16 and had a license, looked at me as if to ask if I wanted him to drive. But I wanted to drive, so we proceeded to Cape Cod, with me behind the wheel. It seemed perfectly normal and reasonable to me. Plus, I had "General Nuisance" and the Registrar of Motor Vehicles in the car with me, so what could possibly go wrong? It was fun for me, and we made it safely to the base, although the guards at the gate of the base look very surprised when I pulled up.

When I was a little older and was brave enough to question or challenge my father, I would ask him about his habit of breaking the rules and laws. He always told me that rules did not apply to him. Why? Because he was the big General.

When I was commissioned a second lieutenant in the Marine Corps, I sometimes followed in his entitled footsteps. I felt that I was entitled to those same privileges. That was a big mistake, and caused me many problems, initially. Later in life I learned, with the help of a therapist, that people get feelings of entitlement from misplaced feelings of our youth that we wanted but never received. I believe it can also be taught, as it was to me by my dad.

Entitlement is running rampant in our country today. If you would like to share your thoughts about entitlement with me, please go to www.terrysweeney.com and let me know your thoughts, and I will share them on my blog.

CHAPTER TWENTY-EIGHT
Respect

"If you want to be respected by others, the great thing is to respect yourself. Only by that, only by self-respect will you compel others to respect you." – Fyodor Dostoyevsky

I don't know how many of you can relate to this, but for many years I hated myself. I had many reasons for these feelings of self-hatred. I'm guessing a lot of it stemmed from my upbringing with dysfunctional alcoholic parents, which in turn led to my enormous consumption of alcohol and pot that poisoned my mind, heart, and body on a regular basis. Mind you, my parents never forced me or any of us to drink or smoke pot. However, my siblings' and my actions, especially drinking booze at a young age, was never condoned either. But, for whatever reason, I had a hard time even looking at myself in the mirror, after a bout with booze the night before.

I compensated by demanding respect from others. By now, I was a 1st Lieutenant in the Marine Corps and got angry with even little things. My anger just hid the fact that on the inside, I was a having trouble. I had no self-respect. And I had little to no respect for others— especially those who were in authority, which made life even more difficult for me, being in the Marines and having to take orders from higher command.

In my opinion, most young people today show very little, if any, respect for others, especially their elders. I think deep down it may be for the same reasons. They have a lack of respect for themselves, or even self-hatred.

They just haven't figured *it* out yet.

As just one example, I recently had some friends over one night to watch a movie. One of the guys let his younger brother and his girlfriend tag along. She is sixteen years old. As we were going through all the movies that I own with the guys, we came across the movie, The Princess Bride, which everyone loves. This young girl took the movie from one of my friends' hands, handed it to me, and said, "Put this in." "Pardon me! How about something like, would you please put this movie in," I said. She replied. "What, this is the one *I* want to watch."

She's 16! I was completely blown away by the disrespect of this child. If that is the attitude of 16 year-old-kids today, are we in deep trouble. Again, none of that happened in my house. Just ask any one of my children.

I think my disrespect stemmed from my father's alcoholism. He was a General in the Air Force and then Air National Guard. According to him, he was the only Air Force General ever who never went to college, outside of Chuck Yeager. That fact alone had to have inflated his ego big time. It seemed to me that people junior to him in the military were constantly kissing his ass. He had a Sergeant working for him. I think his name was Kenny, who was just a super guy. One of his jobs, if you will, was to take the Sweeney kids to a place called *John's Pond* in Mashpee, MA., near the base. In essence he was our babysitter on most weekends. I am not sure that was in his real job description, when he signed up for the Air Guard. However, I do remember that years later he did become an officer. Was that because he did favors for my dad, or did he go to college himself to earn his promotion? I do not know the answer. What I do remember is him having these huge black inner-tube things for us to ride in the water. We could not get enough of that.

At home, we didn't understand why everyone fawned over my father just because he was a General. In fact, behind his back, my brother and I called him "General Nuisance." We wondered why people thought he was so special. He certainly hadn't done anything special for us—except the one year when I got a bike for Christmas. I rode it all day in the snow.

That was a blast!

I was recently talking to a judge I know here in town. She told me that when she gets home, nobody cares who she is either or what she does, and they certainly do not stand up when she walks into a room. I guess that was the way it was with "General Nuisance" as well.

To me, he was just the man in authority who would come home drunk, yell at us, and then ignore us. He was never really there for me, which he admitted later on in life. I didn't think I owed him any respect. In fact, I remember sitting in the breakfast room one morning. It had been snowing all night and it was still snowing. I just knew we were going to get the day off from school and was listening to the radio for our school to be mentioned. I looked out the window as I ate breakfast and saw a tow truck towing my father's staff car into our driveway. I turned to my mother and asked, "Why is there a tow truck pulling dad's car into the driveway?"

She told me that he had parked it on the neighbor's lawn the night before, and the neighbors were pissed.

"Oh," I responded. Things like that didn't strike me as very strange. That type of behavior was the norm at our house.

The odd, strange, and outlandish behavior portrayed by both of my parents was just what we knew. In fact, it seemed like most of our friends' parents were the same way. So, it made sense that we had very little dignity or respect for my parents, our teachers, or for myself. The one difference was that you could never talk to somebody older than you with disrespect. You might not have respected their behavior in your heart, however you better have shown respect when addressing your elders, unlike this 16-year-old kid.

I have also told you in a previous chapter the story of the time that my dad brought a rainbow of colors of paint home and encouraged me and my siblings to paint over my mom's beautiful newly-painted kitchen. I cannot fathom the thinking process and effort this sick man went through to get to this plan of action. All of this affected me. I obviously did not have any respect for my father. And what about me? Where was my dignity and self-respect?

I didn't have any.

Eventually, I ended up going down the road of alcoholism too, just like my old man. It was not until I sobered up that I realized this. I hated, even despised that I had become just like him. I couldn't respect myself. Therefore, how could I possibly respect anyone else.

One of the tools that has helped me to sort out a lot of my thoughts and feelings over the years is journaling or writing. I have been advised not only to have a journal, but to use it well. It does not work if I do not write in it. By putting pen to paper, I am able to more easily identify my feelings and thoughts. Without it, I tend to stray into whatever direction in which I find myself.

I highly recommend journaling or writing as often as you can, maybe every Sunday for example. Take the time, because this part *is* all about you. Writing definitely helps me to stop the "committee" in my head—those thoughts of self-condemnation that kept me trapped in feelings of anger, guilt, or shame. Writing in a journal is a healthy habit, that should be passed on to the next generation. If you aren't willing to write in a journal, ask yourself: Why not? What are you doing on the outside, or feeling on the inside, that is preventing you from looking at yourself through writing?

In my pre-recovery days, I remember a particular Biblical passage in The Gospel of Matthew that always confused me. Matthew 22:34-40 says, *"But when the Pharisees had heard that He had put the Sadducees to silence, they were gathered together. Then one of them, which was a lawyer, asked him a question, tempting him, and saying, 'Master, which is the great commandment in the law?' Jesus said unto him, 'Thou shalt love the Lord thy God with all thy heart, and with all thy soul, and with all thy mind. This is the first and greatest commandment. And the second is like unto it, thou shalt love thy neighbor as thyself. On these two commandments hang all the law and the prophets.'"*

I did not know how to take these verses. How could I love others as myself if I hated myself? How would I know how to treat people, like my neighbors, fellow students, teachers, friends, parents, or siblings? We have to have love and respect for ourselves first, before we can give it to others. That was pretty obvious to me, I just didn't know how to do it.

So, when I finally did get help from my addictions, my sponsor, John, said to me one day, "Terry, I want you to look in the mirror every day and say I love you to yourself."

"I can't do that," I thought to myself. I was working as a stockbroker in those days, so I had to wear a suit and tie to work. Thankfully, I do not have to do that anymore. So, as I was getting ready to leave the house every morning, the thought would cross my mind that if I saw John that day, he was going to ask if I was doing my "mirror work." So, at first, I did not even go into the bathroom. I would stand outside the bathroom, pop my head into the bathroom, look at the mirror, any really fast say, "I love you," barely even looking at myself in the mirror before I took off out the door. That way, if John asked me, I could honestly say that I was doing the work.

I didn't want to lie to him.

I eventually was able to stand in front of the mirror and say, "I love you," however never believed it. But, I stuck with it, day after day. Finally, after about a year and a half of doing this every day, one day out of the blue, I stood in front of the mirror, straight and tall, and said the words, "I love you." And on that day, I believed it! Wow. What a feeling that was for me. Now, it may not take that long for you, but that is what it took for me to finally believe what I was saying to the mirror. Sometimes quickly, sometimes slowly, we say in recovery. I had finally come to a place in my life where I could say to myself, "I love you," and mean it!

I meant it that day because I was consistently *willing* to do the work. That's the key. Just be willing to be willing if you have to. But now, I live a life that allows me to love my neighbor as myself. Praise the Lord!

CHAPTER TWENTY-NINE
God

"The only thing you need to know about God, is that there is one, and you are not it."   – Roy Poulter

When I grew up, I, along with all my siblings, attended a parochial school, St Agatha's, taught by the Sisters of Mercy, however, that was in name only. My religious beliefs, if you want to call them that, consisted of the nuns beating the crap out of the boys. Sister Damian was the worst. She would make us (boys only) put our hands out, while she beat our knuckles with a ruler. In those days, that kind of punishment was perfectly acceptable. And you did not go home and tell your mother what had happened, or she would beat you as well.

Most of the nuns hated me, at least that is the way I felt, being the class clown. There was one exception, Sister

Carlos—my second-grade home room teacher. May God rest her soul. For some reason she loved me, and was not bashful about letting me, or any of the other nuns, know it. She went out of her way to defend me, no matter what I did. Why? I never knew, but what a difference one person can make in your life, especially at such a young age!

I was also an altar boy, so I loved it when there was a funeral to serve, because you got out of classes for a while—an excused absence—and either the priest or the grieving family usually slipped you a few a bucks for helping out with the Mass. They had no idea that the priest saying the funeral Mass, would try to grope us while we were changing back in the sacristy. I never allowed Father Riley to get a hold of me. I would run into the closet where they keep their vestments, putting my back to him. Sadly, though, he did get a hold of some of my friends, and to this day they still struggle with what happened back then. I tell them to drop the rock. Maybe now, they can read Chapter 14 on Forgiveness.

The funny thing about the Catholic church, and often our brothers and sisters in the Jewish community, is that people continue to bash our faiths, set fire to our churches, defecate in, or have sex in our houses of worship. Why? If these "nones" say they do not believe in a God, why go through all this trouble? It's fascinating to me, because I just do not get it. In addition, thousands upon thousands of Catholics have left the church because of the pedophile issue, or so they say, that has been highlighted over the past decade or so. Why? It seems to me that they have put their faith in other people, priests in this example, instead of putting their faith in God, which is what we are called to do. Or maybe, they have always wanted to leave the church, and this scandal was their ticket out.

Interestingly enough, statistics show that the number of pedophile priests, compared to pedophiles in society as a whole, is about half of what they are in the rest of society. However, the liberal media does not report about that. Because it is the Catholic church, they salivate as they report on the bad news in the church. Thank God, that He is the final judge and not us.

Anyway, all I remember was this hell and damnation stuff being taught in grade school. So, by the time I reached the eighth grade, I, too, was done with the Catholic church. I left the church, even though I went to a Catholic High School (Boston College High School) and a Catholic college (Marquette University). I figured that I had done so many things wrong by then that God was already done with me and I was going south when I died. Therefore, why not live life the way I wanted to—to the fullest in my case. And that's exactly what I did from ages 13 to 30. It was pure joy and insanity all at the same time. By the way, Albert Einstein famously said, "Insanity is doing the same thing over and over again but expecting different results."

That is what I was doing. It was insane.

So, when I got to my first official squadron in California, after a year and a half of training, and saw that these guys were just as crazy as I was, I felt like I was at home. It was pure bliss.

Did I really believe that if we masturbated hair was going to grow on our hands? That's what these nuns had taught us. Yes, initially I did. That was until I found out otherwise. As Woody Allen says in the movie *Annie Hall*, "Hey, don't knock masturbation. It's sex with someone I love."

Then there was Dorothy, my mother, who when backing up her car in the church parking lot after Sunday Mass, and getting beeped at, would roll (yes roll) down her window and yell; "Blow it out your ass." Very pious, me mum. Once when I asked my mother if priests could swear, she looked at me and said: "Are you kidding me, they're worse than sailors." No more explanation needed for me.

My parents also loved to entertain. It seemed to me, aside from our own parties, when my parents were gone for the weekend, that at least once a month, they had a party or shin- dig as they call them at our house. Therefore, it was not uncommon to see the local Monsignor, along with his minions, at 277 Adams Street. All drunk by the end of the evening.

This was the *religious background* of my youth. My older brother Chas had a hilarious nickname for every one of the nuns, as well as the lay teachers, all women, who taught at our grade school as well. Our church had an upstairs and a downstairs, enabling consecutive Masses to be going on at the same time, or maybe 20 minutes apart, for the flow of traffic. Times were a lot different back then.

Anyway, I remember during one Lenten season one day my fifth-grade teacher was walking back to her pew after going to Communion. She had her hair pulled back, so her forehead was in full view. It was also very shiny. My older brother Chas leaned into me and said; "Does she simonize her forehead?" I completely lost it during Mass, and got thrown out for laughing, by my mother! The only other time that happened to me, was when my sister Carol-Cakes took me to see the James Bond movie, *Thunderball*. When that boat split apart, I lost it, to which the usher had to come down and give me a warning for laughing so loud. I could not help myself. And I was only ten-years-old, but grateful that my sister had taken me to see such a great picture. I did not want to get thrown out at that point in the picture either. I have a very good sense of humor, which I think is critical, especially when it comes to "God" issues. In fact, I truly believe that God has the best sense of humor of all. For example, why would He give men their sexual prowess between the ages of, say, 19 - 25, and give woman theirs between the ages of 30 - 45, and say, work with it!

When I was just starting out in recovery, either day two or day three, of my 12-step program, the guy who I perceived to be the president of the organization, Roy came up to me after a meeting and said; "Hey, how are you about the God thing?" "Huh?" I asked, with no clue what he was asking me. He then asked me; "Do you believe in God?"

I replied, "Of course, or yeah, sure," or something like that.

He then said, "Man, if you believe in God, you have half

this program licked." I did not know what he meant by that, however what went through my head was, "Wow, I have only been here a few days, and I am half way done already. This is great. Just because I believe in God?" I failed to realize at the time that those folks who do not believe in God, had a much harder time in recovery than I had, because of their lack of belief.

This is what I know and why I love being a Catholic, after being absent for so many years. The Catholic church began *40 days* after our Lord Jesus Christ ascended into heaven—on The Day of Pentecost, to be specific. Throughout the centuries, we have had visionaries and saints, too numerous to count, who have willingly died for this faith. We have had a successor to Peter, who eventually became the first Pope, and died a martyr. In Matthew 16:18, *Jesus said to Simon Peter, "I also say to you that you are Peter, and upon this rock I will build My church; and the gates of Hell will not overpower it."*

So, of all the Christian churches, the Catholic church started in the very first century. I think that is so cool. Other Christian churches such as the Baptists, Lutherans, Methodists, Anglican, Episcopalian, and Presbyterians trace their origins to the Protestant Reformation. Mormonism is a cult, so I've been told, and started around 1830, after some 24- kid named Robert Smith, from Vermont of all places, wrote the book of Mormons. Whatever.

Conversely, the Catholic church is so rich in history and traditions. We also believe that Holy Communion, is the actual body, blood, soul and divinity of our Lord Jesus Christ. That is probably the most amazing thing on this earth! And, I can go to that banquet every day if I want to, and I usually do.

Now, were some of these Popes bad apples? Yes, of course they were. But again, our church does not put our faith in people, who will always fail us. We put our faith in God alone. Anyway, I was early in my recovery now, and I was hearing for the first time in my life talk about a *loving God*. "A loving God? What are these people talking about? The only God I ever knew was the punishing God the nuns had taught us about." But this 'loving God thing' was part of almost every meeting I attended.

I wanted to find out where and how I could find out more about this loving God. I literally had no idea what these people were talking about. My brother Chas and his buddy Jim, had just completed a weekend retreat in Boston, called a *Cursillo*. When he finished his weekend, he called me out in California and said that I had to do a Cursillo as soon as possible. Both Chas and Jim had also been in a 12-step program. In addition, making a *Cursillo* is available to almost any Christian denomination in the US. For young adults, there is a program like Cursillo called Search, however I do not know anything about that or if it is still around. Anyway, it was during my *Cursillo* weekend retreat that I finally met this loving God that everyone had been talking about at the meetings. Now I knew why Chas and Jim insisted I go on one of these retreats. I cannot tell you what that revelation was like in words, other than it was the most beautiful retreat I have ever been on in my life. *De Colores* to all my fellow cursillistas out there.

This is not to say you have to attend a 12-step meeting or attend a Cursillo retreat to find this loving God. I am just telling you what happened to me. Least of all, my brother Chas had everything to do with me attending this weekend in California. Unbeknownst to me, when he found out the weekend I was attending my Cursillo, he and his girlfriend (Tiger Lady) flew out to celebrate with me at the end. It was incredible, and all you cursillistas understand exactly what I am talking about.

My brother, Handsome Chas, of all people. The same guy who taught me how to be a con artist, as well as making me burst into laughter during holy Mass. That Chas!

May God rest his soul.

Author's note: Most people, if you are from Boston, have a nickname. Mine is T-Bird.

CHAPTER THIRTY
Shame

"Those who conceal their sins do not prosper, but those who confess and forsake them obtain mercy."
— Proverbs 28:13 (NAB)

What is shame? In the *Thorndike Barnhart Advanced Dictionary*, second edition, shame is defined in three ways:

1. A painful feeling of having done something wrong, improper, or silly.
2. A disgrace, dishonor.
3. A fact to be sorry about; a pity.

Most people that I know have experienced some sort of shame. Either they have shame for something they are currently involved in, or they feel deep rooted shame for something that they did—or was done *to* them—in the past, shame that haunts them no matter how long ago it was.

But shame doesn't have to haunt us…ever!. Just as our secrets keep us sick, as we discussed in a chapter one, shame can eat us alive if we do not properly recognize and deal with it.

About a year ago, I did something that I regret very much and for which I carried a lot of shame. My niece's wedding was held at the Naval Officers Club in Newport, R.I. It was a beautiful day and she was a beautiful bride. The details of what I did are not important. In fact, I did not even know what I had done until the next day. My sister, who was the mother of the bride, held a brunch for the family that Sunday morning, the day after the wedding. She went to every length and put out quite a spread. It was at this brunch that I learned about my behavior, and what I had done at the wedding. When I found out what I had done, I asked my brother, "Why didn't you stop me?" He looked at me and said, "You were making me look good."

This was true, but not exactly the answer or the support I was looking for.

My oldest sister, Queenie, said, "Terry, it was a real shit show." I believed her. Embarrassed and full of shame, I flew back to Naples, Florida, which was where I lived at the time.

I realized that I had many amends to make to my family members, to which they all agreed.

A few days later I was at my favorite hangout in Naples called the *Parrot*. I was talking to my two best friends from Naples, Michael Dock ("Doc," as we called him) and David Potter. So, I told them what I had done at the wedding. Doc looked at me and simply said, "Own it." These two men are true friends whom I love, and I knew I could be honest with them. They are the type of friends that will tell you to your face, without holding back, when you screw up. They don't sugarcoat anything. These are the type of friends that I treasure. I could care less about my feelings getting hurt. I need to hear the truth, the brutal facts. I would tell them the truth and do the same for them, *no matter what*.

By the way, both of these guys also happen to be great guitar players. We share an appreciation for music, and that is one of the reasons we get along so well. Doc plays in a band called, "The Old 41 Band," and David plays a mean guitar and harmonica, when he is not bar tending at the Parrot. If you are ever in Naples, Florida, I highly recommend going to the Parrot. David is about 6'5' tall, and one of the bartenders, so you really cannot miss him. One super guy.

So, I made my amends to my family. I wrote a letter to my brother and all of my sisters who were in attendance. I let them know how truly sorry I was. I admitted that I was wrong.

I even went to *Sacrament of Reconciliation*—this is confession for Catholics.

Most of my siblings have still not forgiven me, even though it has been over a year since the wedding, which is very sad to me. However, I have no control over them. I did what I needed to do, which was to make amends (see Chapter 16) and clean my side of the street. If they want to continue to have a resentment (Chapter 21), against me, that is their issue, not mine. I can't change the past, but I can apologize and make amend for my actions. That goes for all of us. If we make amends to those we have harmed, which is not easy sometimes, that is all we can do. We cannot change what other people think about us (chapter 2); however, *we can be free*. In fact, I even asked my siblings to pray for me. My brother's reply was, "You use your God as a crutch. Don't you ever push your God on me." Okay then, and I thought he and I had the same God, as we were both raised Catholic. Up until this time, I also thought we were best of friends. The only two boys left, from this huge family that we had. What do I know?

Who could possibly live their lives with shame like this? Yet, many people do. Therefore, if you make mistakes, own them, and then make amends for what you did. If you can't make the amends right away, just be willing to do them. If you're willing to be willing, the proper time will come. Then, you too, will be at peace, knowing that you did all that you could do, leaving the results to God. It is my sincere hope that maybe when my siblings read the chapters on forgiveness, amends, and resentments they will better understand me and where I come from.

But it may never happen. So, you have to be ready for that as well.

After all, in my house, we were all raised in a very abusive and dysfunctional home, and a lot of that anger and resentment, like mine over the years, might stem from my mother's and father's alcoholism. Dot, my mother, died of what we call Irish Alzheimer's disease. She forgot everything but the grudge.

A terrific book came out years ago called, "Healing the Shame that Binds You," by John Bradshaw. In the book he states: "I used to drink, to solve the problems caused by drinking. The more I drank to relieve my shame-based loneliness and hurt, the more I felt ashamed."

I greatly identified with Mr. Bradshaw. Years ago, I would swear off the booze, almost every day. Then the next morning I would find myself unable to look myself in the mirror as I shaved, as I had done *it* again. I lived in that miserable cycle for years.

Therefore, if you feel like you still carry shame, even if it dates back 10, 20, or even 30 years ago, it is my hope that you to will find the healing that I have. As seen in chapter one, healing begins with sharing our secrets. Write it down. Find someone you trust to share it with. It is possible that when you share it, you may be relieved of the feelings of guilt and shame on that very day. It won't be a secret anymore, and you will never have to hold that burden you have carried anymore. And true friends do not judge. They support, help and encourage. And sometimes your vulnerability in sharing your past shame and secrets can help someone else to have the courage to share and let go of their own shame.

I urge you to try it. It will be worth it.

CHAPTER THIRTY-ONE
Isolation and Loneliness

"Don't surround yourself with yourself."
I've Seen All Good People – Your Move, by Yes

When deciding on the title for this chapter, several words came to mind. Should I call it isolation? Should it be loneliness? Should it be hiding, or a myriad of other titles? But no matter the title, the fact is that from time to time we can find ourselves hiding or isolating ourselves from other people, places, and situations.

Many years ago, I had opened up an office in Toronto, or TO, as the locals call it, for the company I worked for. I had been traveling quite a bit for work at this point. It was just a part of the job. While in Toronto, I had to call a colleague of mine, who was in Washington D.C., to discuss a meeting we were to attend the following week. While on the phone we started talking about other things, as well.

In the midst of the conversation, my colleague, Ed, said to me, "You really like being out there on your own, don't you? I mean, you're a real loner, aren't you?"

I did not understand why he said this, or where he got that notion. To me, I was just a traveling salesman, like so many other men and women at the time. So after I got off the phone with him, I took a little time to think about what he said. I asked myself, "Am I a loner?"

When I got home from my trip, I asked my wife what she thought about my colleague's comments. Did she think I was a loner? She answered that she didn't think I was. In addition, she really didn't like Ed.

I am actually an introvert, which shocks many people that I come into contact with, because I am a very outgoing and friendly person in public. I love being around people, especially children, and talking to them, but after a while I prefer to be by myself. It is how I recharge my batteries. I suppose some might call me an "ambivert," someone who has traits of both extrovert and introvert.

What people don't know is that I often choose not to participate in some functions. Sometimes I can feel isolated, even in a room full of people. And over the years, when I did something I wasn't proud of, when I messed up, or when things didn't go my way, I would pull away from others and isolate myself.

More recently, I have lived in Naples, Florida. and Chandler, Arizona, before moving back to where I had planted my roots in Laguna Beach, California. Naples had a huge population of older people, mostly people from the East Coast—New York, Boston, Philadelphia, and New Jersey. These people moved to Florida for retirement. While I was there, I lived in a 55 and older community. I will never do that again! You would have thought it was advertised as 75 and older. I was definitely the youngest person living in the community.

The community was made up mostly of widowers and widows, although there were still many couples, too—on their second or third marriages, and all of whom seemed to have tiny dogs. These dogs must have been trained to be quiet. Or they must have had some secret special dog food, because none of the dogs ever seemed to bark. I would see my neighbors every morning, walking their obediently quiet dogs, while I was out taking my morning walk.

It was so strange.

It wasn't until I moved to a flat in Arizona, and heard a dog bark, that I realized how strange it was in that Naples retirement community. I don't think I heard a dog bark in the three years that I lived there. Weird, but true. But my point is that the people in the retirement community mostly lived alone, with their pets for companionship.

In Arizona, the tendency towards being alone was the same, although it was a much younger population. I personally love the sound of kids playing tag football or soccer outside. It is the sound of pure joy for me. Maybe it brings back good memories of when I was able to do those things too. I even remember when I lived in Helsinki, sometimes I would go home for lunch. There was a schoolyard near where I lived. I could just sit there and eat a sandwich and listen to the fun these kids were having, even if it was in Finnish. But in my Chandler, Arizona neighborhood, about 90% of the population, male and female, lived alone—with their little dogs. I lived alone too, but without a dog. I love dogs. However, I'm done cleaning up dog poop. (NT)

It astonishes me that so many young people choose to live alone these days. Especially women. More and more women, ages 25 to 35, are choosing to live by themselves, with only a pet or two to come home to for companionship. I don't know if it has always been this way, or if it is a more recent thing happening across the country. I do think that it influences the declining birthrate, which is currently at our country's lowest level since 1986.

Do you have any thoughts about isolation and loneliness? Are you, like me, an introvert? Do you like to hide and escape from people at times? I would love to hear your thoughts, opinions and questions on this topic, so that I can share them on my blog. To contact me with your stories, please go to www.terrysweeney.com.

Thank you.

CHAPTER THIRTY-TWO
Attitude

"Be grateful for what you have and not what you deserve." Anonymous

Do you ever need an attitude adjustment? I think all of us need one from time to time. In fact, there is a local morning meeting in my town that is appropriately named, *Attitude Adjustment*. As one of my colleagues, who is also on the professional speaking circuit, tells his audiences, "Attitude is everything," and calls the bible his manual, as in car mechanic manual.

    I believe that more people in this world need to have an attitude of gratitude. I mean, look around. We are so blessed to live in the best country in the world. We have the freedom to go anywhere we want to, whenever we want. We can do anything that we want to, with hard work and perseverance.

Yet many people still find time to complain about anything and everything.

I wish more people were like my friend Tom. He recently said to me, "Terry, you are always preaching an attitude of gratitude. Well, last week I had to file for bankruptcy and my wife asked for a divorce. I've been out of work for three months and I am not eligible for unemployment because I am an outside contractor. My car is about to be repossessed. Yet, I have never felt better in my life." (Maybe because the bills are finally gone, I don't know)

That may sound crazy to some people. But I get it. Obviously, he is aware of the struggles he has ahead of him, but he is choosing to focus on gratitude for what he has, instead of the things he is losing. He inspires me. I don't know if I will ever have the level of gratitude that my buddy Tom has. Just one of those scenarios would be enough for me to lose it. In fact, I definitely did not react peacefully and with gratitude when my ex-wife surreptitiously divorced me. I did not feel gratitude on that day, or for many months thereafter. But gratitude is something I strive for.

I remember when I lived in Helsinki, Finland. It was 1989. There was only one English speaking 12-step meeting each week. It was held on Wednesday evenings, and was made up of Finns and Swedes who mostly wanted to practice their English. It was a super group of great people though. During the meeting one night I mentioned the phrase, attitude of gratitude, during my share. These folks had never heard that term attitude of gratitude before I introduced it to them. They loved it.

A little over five years later, the international convention for this 12-step program was held. It is held every five years at locations all over the world. In 1995 it was held in San Diego, CA. People from all over the world would attend. I attended with a group of friends from Laguna, (about 60 miles up from San Diego). As I looked around the stadium, I noticed, way up in one of the top sections, the Finnish flag. I told my friends that I was going to go up there to see if any of my friends from Finland were there. Just as I turned around to go, without looking I accidently bumped shoulders with another guy.

It was my best friend from Finland.

Coincidence? I think not. I do not believe in them. This was a God thing. There were over 55,000 people in the stadium that night and we just happened to bump into each other the moment after I told my friends that I was going to go looking for him. As we hugged each other, the first thing he said to me was, "Attitude of Gratitude!" It was a very sweet moment and is now a very sweet memory.

In my daily life I try to practice this attitude of gratitude every day, no matter what life throws at me. Some days I am more successful at this than others. Very recently I lost my baby sister. She was only 56 years old. While I am very sad, I also am very grateful that God had seen fit to take her home. She suffered greatly with alcoholism during her life. She never made it to a meeting. She never found recovery from drinking. She never sought out counseling from her childhood with my parents, and, being the baby, she took the brunt of their insanity. When each of us turned 18, we got the hell out of that house. When my mother wanted to divorce my father, she made my sister lie about my father inappropriately touching her, which she told me never happened. She had a hard life. But I know that she is at peace now.

At the time that I am writing this, our world has been turned upside down by this Chinese virus. Many of us are suffering, physically, mentally, emotionally and financially, as our world has changed and we are being forced to live in a different way than we ever have before.

So how is your attitude? Are you angry, depressed, or anxious over the things that are out of your control? Or are you grateful for the things that you do have at this moment?

My remedy for an unpleasant attitude, as I mentioned in an earlier chapter, is to look at the picture on my refrigerator from the weekend edition of the December 28-29 *Wall Street Journal*. When I see the photograph of hundreds of people living in their shanties on top of a waste dump, that had just burnt down, my bad attitude goes up in smoke and I feel grateful for what I do have. We live in the United States of America, and no matter what is going on around us we have a certain level of freedom and prosperity that communist and socialist countries do not have. Try looking at life that way.

Try having an attitude of gratitude and see how much your life improves.

CHAPTER THIRTY-THREE
Self-Image

"He is the image of the invisible God, the firstborn of all creation."   Colossians 1:15

Living in Southern California has really opened up my eyes to what I view as a major problem in our society today. I lived in the Northeast during my first 18 years of life. My daughters now live in the Midwest. And while this particular issue never seemed as prevalent in those areas as it does in Southern California, it definitely is growing, no matter where people live. In Southern California—or the land of fruits and nuts, even the weather is queer at times, as I like say—it is just more out in the open. What is the issue that we see everywhere?

It is the obsession with self-image.

It is unbelievable to me the extent that people will go to pretend that they are someone that they are not. In this day of social media, people have a platform to pretend they have it all. A perfect body. A perfect family. A perfect relationship. A perfect home. A perfect life. By presenting their lives in a good light, in a way that they want it to look to others, they not only fool others, but fool themselves. In my opinion, this self-image extravaganza is an obsession that is taking over people's lives, at least in So. Cal.

The rise of plastic surgery in Southern California is proof of this. People think they will be happier on the inside if they change their looks on the outside. It seems that a large portion of women I know in California have had *at least* one breast augmentation. In addition, as soon as they are done with *it,* they want to show them off to you, as they are so happy with the themselves. I know that sounds odd, but it's true, believe me. Many of these women have had two or three augmentations because they did not feel they got the desired results from the first time through. *Botox* injections are also on the rise among both men and women. I recently talked to a 'doctor' who administers *Botox* injections for a living. He told me that *Botox* is the new methamphetamine. His clients just can't seem to get enough of it. And he loves it because, as most insurance companies do not cover these procedures, it is a cash cow business.

There are endless things that people do today to present the image they want others to see. They wear fake diamonds and try to pass them off as real to show that they are financially well off. They go to tanning salons because they think it makes them look more attractive, when in reality it is harming them. So, they completely ignore the facts that tanning beds are more dangerous than the sun. According to the *American Academy of Dermatology Association*, there is no such thing as a safe tanning bed, tanning booth, or sun lamp.

Despite all these warnings, self-tanning is just one of the many industries that thrives off people's desperate need for positive self-image in Southern California. (Full disclosure: I use to go to these places when I was in my 30s. Maybe that is why my dermatologist is digging craters in my nose now!)

All of this seems strange to me. Funny, even. But I guess it is just a result of the society that we live in today. Women are told today that, even though they have had children, their bodies should look different, thinner, and more toned, as if they had never carried a child for nine months. Society and especially Southern Californians say people should always be happy. We should never be burned out, too tired, or too inconvenienced. Society tells us that if you have a perfect home, a perfect car, and a perfect body, then you have it all.

We live in a society that says children are too expensive. I remember I was with my dad one time at *Wollaston Golf Course*, a private golf course, known to the locals as Wally World. As we were leaving, this guy who happened to be a doctor in town, said to my dad. "Charlie, how many kids do you have now?" My dad replied "nine." (My baby sister had not arrived yet.) The doctor then said, "How can you afford all those children?" My dad replied, "Doctor, I couldn't afford the first one." Even as a kid, I remembered that line from my dad. It's probably why my wife and I had 6 children of our own. We couldn't afford the first one!

A little digress here: When my mother was going to the hospital to have her last child, I begged and pleaded with her to bring home a boy. There were already too many girls in our house. I was six. "Okay" is all she said. When she came home with another girl, I was angry. "How could you do that *to me*," I asked her. She then told me that they didn't have any girls left, so she had to take a girl. "But next time, I'll make sure to get a boy." To herself she was saying 'Over my dead body.' To me it made perfect sense.

Back to my point. We live in a society that worships money as a false god. The more money you have the happier this idol promises that you will be. It's all a big lie! Just ask anyone who has lots of money. Very few of them are happy. I know, as I was a stockbroker in this very rich town. These people had a lot of dough, but they weren't very happy people. I have a good friend who spends about two hours at the gym each day, sculpting her body, trimming off every ounce that she feels doesn't belong, and striving for a perfection that doesn't exist. Yet, she is always complaining about never having time for her children. Now, I'm not saying that exercise, rest, and a healthy diet are not important, because they are. But maybe if she stopped whining, and started prioritizing her kids over her perfect appearance, then she would be happier. Just saying.

The newspapers in Southern California also have countless advertisements for plastic surgeries, such as breast augmentation and liposuction. The sports section is filled with ads for penile enhancements. One of my good friends told me that his ex-wife wanted to go with their daughter and for the two of them to get breast augmentations. She thought it would be the ultimate mother/daughter bonding experience and a perfect gift for her daughter's high school graduation. Are you kidding me? An 18-year-old girl? Luckily, my friend did not agree to this, so his daughter was exempt. I did not ask about what the ex-wife did, however I am fairly certain I know the answer.

What was this woman thinking? Can she think?

When my daughters were young, and I would see them looking at the glamorous pictures on the covers of fashion magazines in the check-out isle of grocery store, and I would make sure to tell them that the pictures were not real. The photos of models had been airbrushed and the camera was angled for the best shot, while a fan was blowing in the background, pretending to be wind in their hair. In the real world, without professional makeup and lighting, they looked nothing like that. And they certainly wouldn't look like that after having children or when they reached their 40s and 50s–

–without the help of plastic surgery. It is scary how some young girls grow up thinking that the goal is to emulate the ladies on the cover of a magazine.

Why can't we just be who we are?

Well, I'm here to tell you that you can. I know I am. I know my children are, even now that they are adults. Why do we need to have elective procedures done to modify our appearance, instead of accepting ourselves as we are, and letting nature take its course? Is it a question of acceptance, low self-esteem, or insecurity? I'm not sure. These procedures are now just as prevalent for men as they are for women; minus the breast augmentations.

I believe that people should learn how to accept themselves as they are (see chapter 6 on *acceptance*). If you are having an issue with your self-image, just remember that your loving Creator made you in His image and likeness, as you are—not as society "says" you should be.

If you have any thoughts or experience on the subject of self-image, I would love to hear from you. I enjoy finding out why people do what they do, and why they find it difficult to be themselves. I think it would make a great topic for my blog. So please contact me at www.terrysweeney.com.

Together, I hope that we can help others to understand that they are beautiful just the way they are. Thank you in advance for taking the time to share your experience so that others can better cope. It's really great that you do that.

CHAPTER THIRTY-FOUR
Life

"I am the Light of the world. Whoever follows me will not walk in darkness but will have the light of life."
– John 8:12

Life is a funny thing. There are many things that people say or have said about life over the years. The best description of life that I have ever seen was something I first saw in a cemetery on a gravestone. Like most gravestones, it had the person's name at the top, the date they were born, a dash, and then the date that they died. Folks, that dash is NOW! What are you doing with your life right now? Is it what or where you want to be? After seeing these grave sites, on the drive home I told my wife at the time that when I died, I wanted her to have inscribed on my tombstone, "Cause of death—Life."

There have been many volumes of books, movies, even songs written about this thing we call life. Some of my favorites are:

- *It's a wonderful life.*
- *I'm on strike from life.*
- *Life is simple; we make it complicated.*
- *Life is a joke and we're the punchline.*
- *Live life to the fullest.*
- *Life could be a dream.*
- *Life goes on.*

And the list goes on and on.

How long do we have left with this life of ours? The latest actuarial tables used by insurance companies estimate that the average male in the United States will live until the age of 68. The average female will live until the age of 77. These numbers may change, if the Chinese virus continues to run rampant, with many dying before what we would consider to be "their time," yet we live in a time where there are more centurions alive today than in the history of civilization. If you subtract 15 to 20 years of life that was spent in school and in childhood, based on the average age of death, we are left with an estimated 50 to 60 years of really "living" on earth. That, my friends, is not a lot of time. You folks with grandchildren, such as myself, know exactly what I mean. My how fast time is flying by.

In the grand scheme of things, we really don't have a great amount of time here on earth. Many people accept this fact and then strive to make a difference with this life that they have been given. But, in my opinion, most people don't. They accept what is given to them, and then roll with the masses. If you want to change that, re-read chapter 26 on goals and the power of the subconscious mind.

To me, there is something truly miraculous about life. When a child comes into the world, there is no question that he or she is a miracle from God. I know that the most precious and beautiful thing I have ever witnessed, other than looking at pregnant woman, was the birth of each of my own children. My father never had that opportunity, as you were not allowed into the hospitals for this, back in the old days. When physicians in training go to school and study the anatomy of human the human body, these students get to see how fascinating the insides of a human life actually is. When physiologists look into the workings of the brain, or the normal functions of living organisms and their parts, they are in awe.

I once had the opportunity to view an autopsy when I was about 19 years old. One of my good friends, Kenny, was studying to be a physician, and this day he had to observe an autopsy. So, he invited the gang to come along and watch with him. Only about half of the guys wanted to go, however I would not have missed this chance for the world. And sure enough, it was as fascinating as I expected it to be. The human body is one incredible thing.

I also remember hearing of a woman, a few years back, who lived in a nearby town, who died in her sleep at the age of 35. The autopsy showed there was absolutely nothing wrong with her. The cause of death remained a mystery. Meanwhile, on the same day, about one mile away in the same town, a small child was run over by a car—*twice*.

That child walked away from the accident without a scratch.

So, life is definitely a mystery to me. (Or as Roy Orbison would say: She's a Mystery to Me, on his Mystery Girl album). It cannot always be explained. All we can do is take this life that we have been blessed with and do something meaningful with it.

This is what I am attempting to do by writing this book. I have certainly had what I call, "my turn in the barrel." I have had my low points, my failures, my depressions, my addictions, and more. But I am willing today to live life on life's terms, which for me means taking my medications as directed. Because along with the bad, I have had a lot of good things in my life also. And I have learned that life *is* definitely worth Living. And for my dear friends who from time-to-time, might contemplate suicide, as I did for so many years. To my brothers and sisters who may be thinking about suicide, from time-to-time, as I once did, please, please do not take your life away from us. You are way too precious for that. In addition, even if you do not believe in any type of God, please know that God loves you more than anything, and I mean anything, in the world. His dying on the cross for you, yes for you, is great testimony. I remember a guy at one of those fellowship meetings told me early on, "Terry, even if you were the only person on earth, God would have died on the cross for you." Bang! That is the one line I live by every day. Do you know why? Because it's true.

Everyone, and I mean everyone, has their turn "in the barrel."

My friend Billy is the one who coined that term, "my turn in the barrel." What he actually said was, "We all have our turn 'in the barrel' every one of us. It's what you do with your life when it is your turn in the barrel that matters." The truth is, we do not stay in the barrel forever. In fact, once we walk though, whatever it is, we actually become a stronger and better person for it. Again, my friends, DO NOT give up, when it is your turn in the barrel.

One of the hardest things a parent has to teach a child, in my opinion, is that life isn't fair. I believe that sometimes that concept is even harder to grasp as adults. For some reason we have the notion that we have to have our share. That we don't deserve the natural consequences of our actions. That we shouldn't have to suffer. (Where did that one come from?) That is just not the truth. We all have to suffer in this life, some more than others.

The thought that some people hold to that we are not supposed to suffer in any way perplexes me. I'm not sure where this belief comes from. I believe that we are all called to suffer. As for me, I have chronic back pain. I have had numerous surgeries. I've had acupuncture to epidurals. I have titanium rods in my back, after I had to eject from an RF-4. When it comes to procedures to alleviate back pain, you name it, I've had it. What I don't have is access to incredible surgeons to fix me, as the greats like Tiger Woods do. Tiger Woods had amazing surgeons that got him back from incredible injuries to his back and knees to winning the Masters Tournament… again! It was an incredible feat to even get back to playing the game of golf again, much less playing competitively, to winning the Masters Championship. In my experience, after the very first surgery on my back, it is a very hard recovery, involving physical therapy for another six to eight months. I do not think people realize what Tiger has had to go through, just to stand up again. And there he was putting on the green jacket. Just incredible!

My hope, friends, is that by reading my experiences, strength and hope throughout my life, you too can experience the freedom necessary to live life on life's terms as well. No matter what comes your way you can overcome your struggles and hardships and embrace the goodness and blessings of life with an attitude of gratitude.

I sincerely hope at the end of each chapter that you have taken the time to stop and reflect how that particular topic applies to your personal life. I hope that you go back and, if you haven't already, do some writing or journaling as you reflect on each chapter. A new life *will* grow if you just have the willingness to be willing.

Ask our Lord to help you with your shortcomings too. We all have character defects, parts of us that we have twisted and warped into things that are destructive to ourselves and others. But God can help us to take these character defects and turn them into assets.

Your experience with your struggles and hardships can someday help others in ways that you can't even imagine. Your darkest past can be another person's ray of hope. Therefore, take the steps necessary to change your life, the way you want it to be, so that you can help change the lives of others. Live life to the fullest so you can really make a difference. Take a stand. Be humble. Don't be judgmental or prejudiced. Instead, be patient, loving, and tolerant. Learn to accept people, places and things as they are. Let go of control. Pray.

May God bless each and every one of you. Finally, no matter what you or I do, God still loves us. He cannot *not* love us. This is the truest blessing of life, just knowing that we have that love from the person who made us. That's pretty cool. And, if all else fails, try following the *Pet Shops Boys* hit song and …Go West!

EPILOGUE

The silence was deafening after Toby and Ali moved out of the apartment. It had been a long time since anyone had lived with me after my divorce. They cooked and cleaned, which I loved—and we loved to dance. They would blast the music on my surround-sound stereo system (21 Pilots mostly), then party some more. It was fun; however, it did take away from my writing time. In addition, having already raised six children, four of whom are girls, it was odd to feel responsible for two more young woman, even though they were both in their twenties.

Both women had been thrown out of their homes, Ali, because at 17, she had gotten pregnant, and was forced by her mother to have an abortion. Toby, by her father, a staunch Mormon, because she had the gall to have her best friend, a boy, over to her house, when her parents were out one evening. So, when she was "caught," she was thrown out of her home, even though she has mental health issues, is gay, and both of them were fully clothed when "caught". Really? I told Toby's father that I would NEVER, could NEVER throw any one of my daughters out of the house at age 18, no matter what they did! That was the end of that short relationship. And speaking of Mormons, did you folks know that on that in May of 2020, the State of Utah, where the majority of Mormons live, under the guise of this Chinese virus, unanimously passed a bill that lowers polygamy from a third-degree felony to a minor misdemeanor, like a traffic ticket. That is very scary stuff to me!

Neither of these girl's parents would allow them back into their homes, even as this new Chinese virus was starting to overwhelm the country *and* the rest of the world. I did the only thing I know how to do in such situations. I prayed to our Lord for help, and asked one of my daughters, Siobhán to pray for me and for them, as well. Our Lord replied to me in kind with a very simple message: "Just show them that they are loved." That was easy for me, as they were both so adorable and lovable. They reminded me of my own girls, just very sweet.

When I got back to writing *Pearls*, things had changed. I had changed.

I no longer viewed this book as simply sharing my experiences, strength, and hope with you. It became more than just passing along the wisdom that was so gently passed down to me over all these years, especially by John, Roy, and Howard. As it turns out, the book turned into a follow-through or follow-up book if you will. It became about trying to help each other become better people, overcoming the obstacles that can and do hold us back from being the best people that we can possibly be.

For example, let's just take a look at chapter 17, the one about *insecurity*. I came to believe that with the power and tools of the Internet, it is very possible that through my website, www.terrysweeney.com, we could have a life-line for helping each other. I have asked my readers to share their experiences, strength, and hope, and not just for those who have a tremendous amount of insecurity. It would be great to hear from those of you who did have an insecurity problem, or any problem we discussed in the book and how you overcame that obstacle.

This way, my staff can compile that information and blog about it on our website. Let's all help each other!

I have asked you in several chapters to write to us so we can connect you with those people who have overcome the same obstacles and hopefully help others do the same. This second part is very exciting for me, knowing how our Lord can and does work though all of us, whether you believe in God or not. I've mentioned earlier that life is so much easier, when we do believe in God AND trust in His intercession always. To paraphrase Saint Bernard of Clairvaux; "Death's author has already been defeated. Let's all bloom again by the grace of a new blessing."

Finally ladies, for you that are unmarried listen to the U-2 song from the Joshua Tree album that sings, *I Still Haven't Found What I'm Looking For.*" LOL

Peace to All of You – Terry Sweeney

ABOUT TERRY SWEENEY

In the year that Dwight Eisenhower was re-elected President, Congress approved the Highway Act, which allowed for construction of the U.S. interstate highway system and Elvis Presley's had two number one hits, *"Don't Be Cruel"* and *"Hound Dog"* for eleven weeks in a row, I was born.

I was the eighth child, having lost a brother and sister before I was born, of what would eventually be 12 children, to then Col. Charles W. Sweeney and Major Dorothy Sweeney. My father was the pilot who dropped the second atomic bomb on Nagasaki, Japan, ending the Second World War.

I was born at St. Margaret's hospital in Boston, MA., went to Catholic schools, eventually being commissioned a second lieutenant in the United States Marine Corps upon graduation from college. I spent nearly seven years of active duty, and two years of reserve duty with the Marine Corps, flying F-4 or

RF-4 aircraft, as a RIO, out of El Toro, CA., until I left the military to become a stock broker in 1988.

At the age of 34, I married and had six beautiful children with my then wife, two boys and four girls, who are all now adults. My wife divorced me after 25 years of marriage, so I'm currently single…but looking (haha). I worked other jobs, mostly in the health care industry, before starting my own company 20 years ago, assisting people who had leveraged too much debt into reasonable payment solutions.

I am currently retired in Laguna Beach California, where I write books for a hobby. When I am not writing—and even when I am—I always have music playing on my surround sound home theater network, from the 50s jazz and blues era through the 90s and the pop rock era. Music, for sure, is my love and passion, and feel extremely blessed to have been brought up in the best time ever for musical artists.